How To Play Dodgeball

This Handbook Belongs To:

How To Play Dodgeball

FUNDAMENTAL TIPS & TECHNIQUES TO IMPROVE
YOUR GAME, HAVE MORE FUN AND WIN!

By John Clinebell

Taxiwax Publishing
Los Angeles, California

ISBN-10: 172493354X
ISBN-13: 978-1724933546

Library of Congress Control Number: 2018909448

Photographs by Jessica Star
Book design by Greg Gubi

Printed in the United States of America

HowToPlayDodgeball.com

CONTENTS

for my favorite sport in the world

FOREWORD

As you read this book, it will become evident that the proceeds from this stack of ink-filled papers serve only to make me filthy rich. With each page turned, please note two things: your dodgeball mindset will Phoenix from the ashes of yer porn-filled search history into fully empowered form, and my Percocet prescriptions will be one step closer to being paid for in cash.

In life you become what you practice. If you practice shoving bananas into the tailpipes of Hyundai Sonatas then over time you will be an expert at Hyundai tailpipe banana shoving. But if you finish reading this literary apothecary on dodgeball, you will begin to understand the spherical arts. By the second read, you will realize everything you see has become circular. The third read will make you all that is dodgeball. Prepare yourself... This is your dodgeball becoming. Drink lots of fluids!

- David Benedetto

PREFACE

I was hooked the moment I heard, back in 2006, that adults with maybe some screws loose were playing pickup dodgeball in a gym in Hollywood each week. Didn't take long before I'd had my first kiss with an 8.5" red rubber ball to the face. Had to stand outside a while and feel that black 'n' blue sting. Quickly learned to avoid rocket shots to my junk. Through the pain and adrenaline, I eventually discovered that I could hang. Sometimes more than hang. Like dodge throws. Gun out targets. Sometimes even catch the best arm in the gym to end a game. These days, it feels badass most of the time to play dodgeball. In my own unique way, I'm a force to be reckoned with by the other team. That's how it should be!

The idea for this book is so simple. I wrote it so you don't have to suck as long as I did at playing dodgeball. You can avoid the rookie mistakes I made. I don't want you flapping helplessly around out there. Catching like a leaky diaper, and throwing like a wetnap. I'm confident that if you apply the techniques I suggest, over time you will emerge victorious on the court.

Here are my recommendations for getting the most out of this book:

1. Read this book with a pen and highlighter handy. Some sections of the book will seem "duh" level obvious to you, yet other portions will make you almost wet yourself after

reading. Those moments are the ones you wanna draw Q*bert and unicorns next to so you notice them more quickly on future readings.

2. Practice these skills on the court. It doesn't do a lick of good to know this stuff in your head if you aren't willing to give it a shot during a game. Dare to jump over balls coming your way. Have the audacity to snipe crosscourt when you think the chance is there. Find the nerve to act aggressive, even if it's not in your nature. I promise you, breakthroughs will happen if you can throw out everything you think you know about playing dodgeball and simply trust that what I'm saying works.

3. Reread this book! You will definitely not soak in all the valuable knowledge these pages contain on first inspection. Highlight what really speaks to you, talk about it with your teammates, put the book on a shelf... then pick it back up again after you've had some time to practice. You'll see what techniques you've forgotten about and some you were not ready to add to your war chest when you first bought the book.

I also have to acknowledge that there are some people who read this book that play in recreational leagues and don't care about being a badass out there. If you're along for the ride just to get some entertainment and maybe learn a couple things in a less serious fashion, then that's great too. The more the merrier!

So congrats and thanks for reading the preface. It's often the worst part of a book. Page filler that people skip. Since you're smart and read mine, you're now fully prepared to begin your journey to becoming one bad mofo with a red ball in your hand.

- John

DODGEBALL HISTORY

I don't remember how many million years ago. Many. Then something about primordial ooze. Then apes with slings flinging feces at walls. Montage of Neanderthals picking berries, quickly rubbing dead rats against each other to make a fire, and taking the most sacred of squats. Medium-angle shot of men and women who have never showered huddled around a raging fire as a howling wind batters the cave entrance. Then the wheel. Two eagles making sweet love whilst midair slam into a tree. Lightning strikes the tree and then the first rubber ball thuds to the ground. Then "Dodgeball" the movie.

Since then, dodgeball has become the #1 American pastime*, a treasured Olympic sport*, and pretty much rules every aspect of today's modern athletic landscape*. Oh, dodgeball, you've come a long way.

* Not actually true. Although I certainly hope all these things come true by the time the Second Edition is released.

THE BASIC RULES OF DODGEBALL

MAIN GOAL OF IT ALL: The first team to send the other team's entire squad to the out line wins the game.

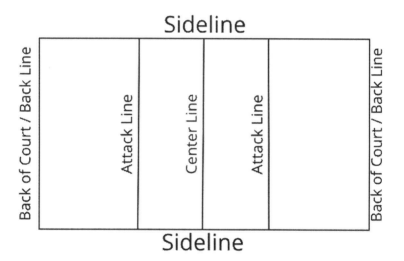

The game usually takes place in an old and gross-smelling gym. Balls are lined up on what is called the "center line." This line separates the court exactly in half. Players line up on opposite sides of the court, make faces at each other, and await the start of the game. Someone usually yells "dodgeball" to kick things off. Once the game starts (this is called the "opening rush"), players run to the center of the court to secure balls. First come, first served. Then people start to fire away.

DODGEBALLISM: *"OPENING RUSH"* - the initial action that takes place when teams run for the balls at the center line at the start of a game of dodgeball.

If a thrown ball hits someone and then hits the ground or a wall, that player is out. Once a player is out, they go to what is called the "out line." The first person to get out is first in the out line, the second is the second person in line, and so on.

DODGEBALLISM: *"OUT LINE"* - a line up of players who are out of a dodgeball game. Each team has its own out line. It starts with the first player to get out and ends with the most recent player to get out.

If a thrown ball is caught by someone, whoever threw the ball goes to the out line, and the player in the front of the catching team's out line comes back into the game.

DODGEBALLISM: *"CENTER LINE"* - the horizontal line that runs directly in between the two teams on the court

If you cross the center line for any reason, you go directly to the out line.

A ball is deemed "dead" when it hits the court, a wall, or some ceiling-area obstruction. The ball becomes live again once a player picks it up.

DODGEBALLISM: *"DEAD BALL"* - a ball that has hit a wall or the floor, or someone's head (in a lot of leagues). A dead ball no longer can be caught or get anyone out.

THE SPIRIT OF DODGEBALL: UNWRITTEN RULES

The Honor Code

In an ideal world, no refs are needed to play dodgeball. When everyone is honest, they willingly (although usually not enthusiastically) raise their hand and exit the court when they are hit. People also assume that the other side plays honestly and treat them as such when a close call arises. This is altruistic sportsmanship at its best. Definitely something many leagues espouse in their rule set.

Don't Be a [insert your favorite insult here]

Don't be a dick, don't be a douche. However you call it, it's the same premise. Act like a gentleperson when you're playing. Don't tee off against someone who sucks when they are standing like two feet in front of you. Don't yell at people on the other side of the court even if you think they should have gone out. Take the high road. A friend of mine once told me if you can't do something in a game with a good-hearted smile on your face, simply don't do it.

Dodgeball Karma

This is the idea that what goes around on the court comes around. Paybacks can be a bitch. This goes hand in hand with being a good sport; for those who aren't, it tends to catch up with them sooner rather than later. It works like this. People don't like playing with jerks. Cheaters never feel satisfied with winning no matter how much they win, so their souls are full of hollow sadness. And if you accidentally peg that girl you like in the face because you're throwing out of control... good luck getting that number!

PREPARING TO PLAY

Dodgeball is an intense sport. Understatement of the year perhaps? Even if you're just planning to play in a casual league, a streak of unexpected competitiveness may overcome you once the adrenaline rush of dodgeball game action hits you. Let's cover some things that will keep you safe & injury free.

DODGECHANICS PRO TIP

ALWAYS WARM UP, STRETCH, AND HYDRATE BEFORE PLAYING IN A GAME

Warm Up & Stretch

Getting your body ready to play before a game is not an option. Even if it's just for a few minutes, absolutely make sure to stretch your legs and throwing arm. Side stretches are also key. If your muscles and ligaments aren't warmed up well, they will be much more likely to tear. If you don't know the different kinds of stretches, there are millions of instructional routines out there on the interwebs. Ten minutes of stretching before the game. Period.

As far as warm ups go, it's critical to at least warm up your throwing arm by tossing a ball around with a friend or solo against a wall. Start with light throws and then work your way up until you're throwing at around 80%. Then I like to unleash a couple of peak-level throws, but no more than that before the game starts. Don't want to burn your arm out before the game even begins.

Hydrate

It takes time for your body to absorb water that you drink. And trust me, you will need plenty of water when playing dodgeball. So make sure you are not thirsty a half hour before the game starts. And if you're playing dodgeball for a couple of hours, I would bring at least a two-liter bottle of water with you. You may not drink all of it during the games, but your body will need to rehydrate well after the action is over. So you'll have post-game water. What happens if you don't drink enough water? You can get nasty muscle cramps or pass out from heat exhaustion. If you haven't had muscle cramps before, they are the worst. You will dodge them, with water.

Know Your Limits

Hardly anyone records dodgeball action. I guarantee you, your diving play will not make SportsCenter. I see them just about every game and have yet to see any on ESPN. You don't make your income from playing a rec game. So why give it 110% out there and act like your career depends upon it? Because dodgeball can give you such an adrenaline surge, and you get caught up in it. If you let that go unchecked and you don't have the athleticism to support the things you want to try and do on the court, you will probably put yourself in a position to get hurt. So if dodgeball is the one thing that gets you off the couch each week, don't blow your arm out!

Protective Gear is Your Friend

You'll notice that dodgeball players wear a variety of equipment like finger tape, gloves, compression sleeves, goggles, and knee pads. A lot of this stuff simply gives you an advantage on the court but most of it also protects the body. There's no set of rules on gear. Depending on your play style, over time what makes sense for you will become obvious. Try combinations out and see. The first things people tend to go for are knee pads and finger tape.

Finger tape can help you grip the ball better while providing some basic protection to your fingers and fingernails. Just plain rolls of athletic tape are fine for this. I find it most helpful to tape the thumb, pointer, middle and ring fingers. Just a couple times around each finger, not too tight.

Knee pads allow you to get down to your knees quickly without destroying them. You'll want to get the ones without hard plastic coating as those can trash the gym floors. And err on the side of more padding vs. less.

Listen To Your Body

Our human bodies have an amazing ability to tell us when we are on the cusp of injury. It can start as just a slight twinge of pain or an unusual amount of tightness in a muscle. Practice listening to what your body is telling you when these things happen. When your body tells you something is off, back off. Trust me, it can make the difference between sitting out the rest of a match and going to the hospital.

Be Calm

Sounds like a ludicrous thing to do while playing dodgeball? A calm and even demeanor can save your body from unnecessary stress and strain. Emotions can get the best of us, but when something bad happens to you or your team on the court, just let it roll off your back. Reacting to it can cause you to overexert your body, going past your personal limits and into the potential injury zone. And it just stresses you out unnecessarily.

Breathe

An often overlooked aspect to the recreational gamer. Dodgeball is a physically demanding sport, one that can leave you easily winded. When the action heats up, make sure to keep breathing deeply. Breath is the fuel to your game-winning fire... get ready to feed it constantly!

Be Classy

Remember that everyone feeds off of your energy on the court. And what goes around comes 'round. Emotions can get heated, and sometimes it feels like you can't have mercy on anyone to survive yourself. However, you always have a choice of how you conduct yourself on the court, and it's a reality that you have the potential to hurt others with your decisions. If you have the choice of whether to blast someone up high at point-blank range, or to do a quick shovel pass at their feet (that is probably more likely to be effective anyways), the choice that's going to be less likely to injure the opposing player is pretty obvious. If you're a guy, unnecessarily teeing off on girls is another common thing that leads to injuries. And makes you look like a total prick.

Now that you're mentally and physically prepared to play dodgeball, it's time to learn the core fundamentals of the game.

THROWING

Throwing a dodgeball comes naturally to some people. Most of us have to learn the fundamentals of throwing mechanics, experiment with different styles of throwing, and then log in the 10,000 throws it takes to refine a throwing arsenal. Don't worry, I've got your back here. We'll start with a foundation of throwing mechanics.

Basic Throwing Mechanics

Here's the philosophy of choice. Your arm should be along for the ride. It should not generate the power. Your legs, hips, and core generate the power. Don't throw with your elbow locked, which can lead to problems (e.g., expedited atrophy).

**DODGECHANICS
PRO TIP**

USING PROPER THROWING MECHANICS ALLOWS YOU TO GENERATE MORE POWER AND ACCURACY WHEN THROWING. IT ALSO PREVENTS INJURY.

Generating Throwing Power

Obviously, a ball that's going really fast is tough to catch. Typically, the harder you throw, the more likely it is that you will get people out. Also, throwing hard adds an intimidation bonus to your playing that can be exploited in many other aspects of the game, not just offensive. If you are physically strong, that's good. A few other things factor more heavily into throwing power, however.

Forward Motion

The human body, once put into forward momentum, has the capability to generate enormous amounts of transferable energy. Most effective throwing motions are initiated by a swift forward movement on the court towards the center line. Some players will simply initiate a quick step forward, much like a baseball pitcher would from high up on the mound. Others will utilize more of a "Happy Gilmore" style where they run several paces up to the line before delivering.

DRILL SERGEANT SAYS:

YOUR LOWER BODY GENERATES POWER. DO SQUATS AND LEG WORK IN THE GYM TO BUILD POWER.

Use Your Hips

It's a common misconception that people need a strong arm in order to throw wicked fastballs. If you use your hips effectively, not only will it make a strong arm seem even stronger, it will put much less wear and tear on your arm muscles and will integrate your entire body into your throwing motion. Learning to throw while putting your hips into it is essential for anyone who is a "weak thrower." If learning how to do this sounds baffling, it's not tough. Think "Twist and Shout" or "Do the Twist." Once you get the idea of twisting your hips and torso, then you can start to add some power to the motion, and at some point you'll realize that it's totally natural to use your hips. One thing you may want to consider if you're having a really hard time with this is taking a couple of tennis lessons. While volleying in tennis, almost all of your power is derived from using your hips!

Release Point

Where you decide to release your throw can have a major impact on how much power is generated. Experiment and see for yourself. Eventually, you will find the "sweet spot" that leaves your opponent in the most fear.

Dedicated Follow-Through

Another little thing that can pack some extra "oomph" is making sure that you completely follow through with your intent to throw. Completing your throwing motion is important because there is potential energy that can be transferred to the ball the entire time it is in contact with your body. If you're hesitant because of some sort of fear of getting sniped or something else, you won't transfer ALL the energy you can from your body to the ball before it's released. So whenever you throw, if you are clear to throw, make it a point to dedicate yourself entirely to it. Erase that person crosscourt pump faking you from your mind!

DODGEBALLISM: *"SNIPE"* - attempting to throw out a vulnerable player, typically someone who isn't paying attention to you, or is in the middle of their throwing motion.

DODGEBALLISM: *"CROSSCOURT THROW"* - throwing at an opponent at an acute angle, across the width of the court. An example of this is a thrower on the far left side of their side of the court throwing at an opponent who is on the other side but to the thrower's far right.

DODGEBALLISM: *"PUMP FAKE"* - faking you are throwing at a target whether you have a ball or not.

Throwing Styles

Like a pitcher, you should have a few kinds of throws. Use enough variety to ensure success and longevity. Each game is going to present situations where one kind of throw is going to be better than the other. Here are some varieties you should try. Your mileage may vary on any of these styles.

DRILL SERGEANT SAYS:

TAKE A BALL TO A WALL. TRY TEN THROWS USING A DIFFERENT STYLE OF THROWING FROM YOUR "USUAL". THEN TAKE A SHORT BREAK AND TRY ANOTHER STYLE. TRY FIVE DIFFERENT STYLES TOTAL. THEN SPEND A COUPLE OF MINUTES AFTER THINKING ABOUT THE RESULTS, SPECIFICALLY IN WHAT GAME SITUATIONS YOU MIGHT USE THE DIFFERENT STYLES.

Overhand

This throw is often favored by tall people who can utilize the leverage of their height to drive power down through their arms. It's easier to target with because there are fewer muscles you have to control when throwing.

Sidearm

A good choice for beginners who struggle with generating power. It's the most difficult throw type to accurately control, but the easiest to keep fast and low to the ground. You can bend your knees and drop your hips down into the throw. It makes you a smaller target and increases your power. From my experience, sidearm delivery is the easiest type to put spin on; all it takes is a flick of the wrist as the ball is being released. It's also probably the least telegraphed throw since you don't have to plant your leading foot where you are throwing. But you do take up a lot of court space throwing sidearm. And your delivery can take a long time.

Some vets think it's best to play on the side of the court that matches your arm when you are a sidearm thrower. For example, if you're right-handed, play on the right side. This allows you to see the entire court while throwing so you can avoid getting sniped. Also gives you the wing-span breathing room you'll need to actually execute the throw without accidentally punching a teammate.

3/4

Popular throwing style for players of any build. With this style, when you throw, your arm releases the ball while your arm is more or less at a 45° angle above the horizontal plane of your shoulder joint. It's compact, fast delivery are its most attractive features. Tends to put more strain on the arm. Can be a little less accurate than overhand because there are more muscles to control while targeting.

Submarine Throw

The submarine throw is similar to sidearm, but the ball is released very close to the ground, sometimes coming within inches of it. This can either result in a ball that sails up from the release point or one that stays near shin or foot level.

Fast-Pitch Softball Throw

I've only joked around with softball style dodgeball throwing, but I've gotten people out with it on occasion. You have to grip the ball pretty tightly or you'll lose it. Also you have to know when to release it 'cause otherwise it will sail like a mofo. It can be really effective as a throwing style if you master it.

Soccer Throw

This is a throw where you hold the ball overhead with your hands on each side of the ball, then using your hips and body, you toss the ball while holding it with both hands. Yeah, it's just like soccer players throw from the sidelines, except you are not making things easy for the recipient of the throw. I've seen players who are able to quickly nip people in the feet from short distances using this kind of throw.

Discus

Some players hold the ball like a discus and twist around to generate power. Some only twist as far as they can without revolving around completely while others spin around completely after the throw. I've even seen players who spin around completely before releasing the ball. This throw can put you out of balance, though. Only the nimble need apply?

The Frisbee

Some players can flick a ball they are gripping off their wrist like a frisbee. This throw is largely unpredictable since the only way to make it is by tightly gripping the ball, contorting its shape. And you're usually putting a ton of side spin on the ball. I know some players who are scarily accurate with it though. What they'll do is powerfully spin their body around and then release the ball towards their target with a downward trajectory. It can really catch you by surprise if you're on the receiving end of it.

Basketball Pass

In certain situations, a quick basketball pass style throw works great. This is recommended in situations where the player you are throwing at is completely exposed and highly unlikely to be able to catch your throw. Since it's very accurate, it can be a great throw when the last player on the other side has fallen down on their stomach, for example, and you are trying to hit them in the back or legs at close range. It can also work in targeting a player's legs and feet when they are at close range. Just make sure not to telegraph you're going to do it, because basketball passes are easy to tip up or catch outright if they are within arm's reach.

What Kind Of Thrower Can You Be?

What is the kind of person you can typically throw out? This is something you'll want to figure out quickly or you will not be a good teammate. Lobbing catches over and over at players who can harness your heat really hurts your team's chances of success.

You can use this section of the book to determine your throwing skill level. Start with the first one and then stop when you've reached a place that seems correct. I'll give tips for whatever stage you're at.

**DODGECHANICS
PRO TIP**

TAKE AN OBJECTIVE LOOK AT YOUR THROWING SKILLS. AN HONEST ASSESSMENT OF HOW WELL YOU THROW CAN GIVE YOU INSIGHTS TO WHAT YOU NEED TO WORK ON TO IMPROVE AS A THROWER AND TEAMMATE.

LEVEL ONE

This person says: "Practically everything I throw is caught by just about anyone. When I can even deliver the ball in the right general direction. Everyone on my team kinda secretly hates me because I guarantee at least one easy catch for the other team every game. Why do I even bother trying?"

You've got to start somewhere, right? Even if you never become a flamethrower, you'll find a niche with your dodgeball throwing if you're willing to invest some time and energy into it. Know that. The first step for you is learning to look out for opportunities that maximize your chances of getting someone out. That's in the next section of the book!

LEVEL TWO

This person says: "Same as LEVEL ONE but occasionally I'll get lucky and snipe someone who's not looking. I can't consistently get people out with any type of throw in any type of situation."

Change your approach. Vary your throws. Look your enemy in the eyes. Yell something when you throw. Leverage your legs and hips to generate more power. Try some different throwing styles.

After refining your skills, the next step for you is finding out where your throwing skill can be best put to use on the court. Maybe you'll never have a strong enough aim to gun people out who are standing in the back of the court, but you may be able to develop the perfect quick delivery and low aim to consistently snipe players in the feet while you play close to the line. You'll learn all about where to target and opportunities to throw in the next section. And you'll also learn about the different dodgeball player styles later on that will help you figure out where you best fit into your dodgeball team's overall strategy.

LEVEL THREE

This person says: "I'm not a hard thrower but I'm good at throwing low and hitting people in the feet at close range. Or I have some other niche that I can exploit regularly when the opportunity is there. If I try anything other than that, it's all over the place, not a fastball, and highly likely it'll get caught by a skilled player."

Develop your power. Go back to earlier in this chapter and practice those skills until you can honestly say you throw hard enough to not just be an opportunistic killah! Otherwise, you might just be in the perfect place and it's just a matter of figuring out how best you fit into the scheme of the grand ol' game o' dodgeball.

LEVEL FOUR

This person says: "I can throw hard but no one is going to wince when I unwind. I'm sometimes accurate. I still get caught a lot by the best players and it's frustrating."

You should make sure that you are doing everything you can to generate power, which was covered earlier in this chapter. If you've truly maximized your power, then you might have hit your ceiling as a thrower. But you can always insert some new tricks like putting spin on the ball or learning to act like an intimidator. You'll learn all about that stuff later in the book. You could also try going back and learning a new throwing style or two so you aren't telegraphing the same KIND of throw every time you cork back to toss it.

LEVEL FIVE

"I throw very hard and accurately, and rarely get caught. But I'm more the "silent but deadly" type of player."

You could use some more intimidation tactics. They will make you even deadlier. We'll cover them all later in the book.

LEVEL SIX

This person says: "The opposing team pays attention whenever I step up to the line. When I fake, even without a ball, the other side anticipates dodging my throw. I'm an undeniable court presence."

Braggart. Why are you reading this chapter in the first place? Oh yeah, to get the reminder you're already badass. Nice job!

DRILL SERGEANT SAYS:

GET A TIMER AND SET IT FOR TEN MINUTES. HAVE A PEN AND PAD OF PAPER HANDY. WRITE DOWN ALL THE WAYS IN WHICH YOU COULD INTIMIDATE THE OPPOSING TEAM WITH YOUR PLAYING STYLE AND DEMEANOR. DON'T FILTER YOURSELF; FOCUS ON WRITING DOWN AS MANY IDEAS AS POSSIBLE. YOU SHOULD END UP WITH A LONG LIST. WHEN THE TEN MINUTES ARE OVER, CIRCLE THREE OF YOUR IDEAS AND TRY THEM OUT THE NEXT GAME.

Where Do I Throw?

In general, the best place to throw at people is LOW to the ground. This is because it's much less likely your ball will be caught or popped up and caught. This especially rings true for people who lack velocity on their throws. Throwing low also makes it less likely you'll pop someone in the face.

DODGEBALLISM: _"POP UP"_ - a thrown ball that has been deflected high into the air.

While throwing low is usually best, it's sometimes preferable to aim more specifically. This detailed guide is mainly for throwers who have developed the accuracy to be able to target specific areas of the body. If you don't have accuracy yet, I suggest working on the ACCURACY DRILLS that are incorporated into the book.

Shoulders

This is sometimes the best place to aim for if you've got a reasonably strong arm. People don't naturally catch there, yet it's tempting enough for them to try... and more often than not, they fail.

Feet

Aside from the occasional unlucky pop-up that donks off the top of someone's foot, successfully aiming for the feet often results in an out. Aim high? You'll prolly hit them in the shins which is also good. Aim low? It hits the ground. Oh, well. At least it's not a catch! Tall and overweight people usually don't jump well so aim for their feet.

Shins

The shins are hit or miss. If you miss low, chances are you'll hit the feet which is great. Miss high and you're likely to get caught by a skilled player. In the author's opinion, it's better to hit the floor than get caught, so I prefer to aim for the feet when I'm not trying to simply gun someone out.

Breadbasket

Even if you've got a rocket arm, it's not wise to throw at someone's bread basket. That's because it's the place where most people catch the best.

Upper Torso

It's a little less risky to throw at someone's chest level. It's harder for them to create a pocket to catch the ball with their body at that level. Just be aware that some players are good at popping the ball up if it's thrown at them chest-high. And that could lead to you getting caught out.

Headshot

In most rec leagues, throwing a ball and hitting someone in the head doesn't result in a "kill." People tend to take a shitload of offense to getting drilled in the face. These are the reasons we don't throw high, even if it's tempting to do so sometimes.

DODGEBALLISM: *"HEADSHOT"* - a throw that directly hits an opponent in the head.

DRILL SERGEANT SAYS:

GET A ROLL OF MASKING TAPE. GO TO A WALL THAT YOU INTEND TO THROW A BALL AGAINST. HAVE A FRIEND STAND AT THE WALL AND MAKE A TAPE OUTLINE OF THEIR BODY AGAINST THE WALL.

IF YOU DON'T HAVE ANYONE, JUST MAKE A TARGET DUMMY SHAPE WITH HEAD, TORSO, LEGS AND ARMS.

THEN START BY STANDING A FEW FEET AWAY. TARGET ALL THE DIFFERENT AREAS OF THE BODY WITH YOUR THROWS. THEN TAKE A STEP BACK.

REPEAT THE PROCESS UNTIL YOU ARE TOO FAR AWAY TO BE ACCURATE AT ALL. THEN START WALKING FORWARD ONE STEP AT A TIME UNTIL YOU ARE VERY CLOSE TO THE WALL AND TARGETING THE TAPED SHAPE IS EASY BREEZY.

REPEAT THIS ENTIRE PROCESS AS MANY TIMES AS YOU LIKE TO INCREASE TARGETING ACCURACY.

When Do I Throw?

DODGECHANICS PRO TIP

TIMING CAN BE EVERYTHING WHEN IT COMES TO MAKING A GOOD THROW.

When In Doubt, Don't Throw

This is a good general rule. If you don't know exactly where you're going with the ball, it's a waste. And if you aren't decisive with what your intention is with the throw, then you also probably won't put all your effort into it. While you're waiting to throw for real....

Pump Fake!

Probably the most important thing to be constantly doing when you have a ball. Anyone can do this. You don't even need a ball to do it. Pump faking is where you pretend to throw without actually throwing. The benefits of pump fakes are many; it distracts throwers on the opposing side, distracts the opposing team from people on your team who are actually throwing at them, keeps the other side on guard/passive, helps you defend the sides and the line, and adds to your own reign of intimidation over the opponent.

This is key: a good pump fake needs to be *totally sold* in order to elicit a strong response from the target. So you need to completely act like you are throwing. How much you have to sell it honestly depends on the timing of your throw, whether following through too much sets you up for getting countered/sniped, and if you are a strong thrower or not. I've seen, though, that even weak throwers can intimidate people using this technique. One pump fake can send opposing players leaping into the air. Flame throwers who pretend to throw can often make people on the opposing team move around, duck, or cower in indecision.

So pump fake always, but you have to also be willing to throw some of the time when they aren't expecting you to. Every once in a while (maybe once out of every thirty well-sold pump fakes), you should try and snipe someone in the feet or just unload on them.

Strike Like Lightning

When the opportunity does appear, don't hesitate. Take decisive action whether you are throwing alone or with a buddy. It's little milliseconds of doubt that can change your throw from a surefire out into an embarrassing catch.

Throwing With Others

It's much more effective to throw with at least one other person at the same time towards a common target. This is because it's far harder for someone to dodge two throws at once than it is for them to dodge (or catch) one. If you're not in a position where you can throw with someone else, it's generally a good idea to wait until you can at least pair up with someone to target an opposing player.

What's more, a high-energy person should throw with another high-energy person. Low-energy people should throw with low-energy people. High-energy people don't like countdowns. Low-energy people do.

DODGEBALLISM: *"COUNTDOWN"* - an audible countdown typically used to synchronize throws.

Cross-Court Throws

It's sometimes better to throw at someone at an angle as opposed to straight on. It's harder to dodge or block balls coming at you from different directions simultaneously.

DODGEBALLISM: *"BLOCKING"* - using a ball you are holding to deflect an incoming throw.

Throwing Straight Ahead

When you're concerned about maintaining ball control, it can be better to throw directly at your opponent. This is because if you miss, there's a good chance the ball will rebound off the wall and come back to your team. And more opportunities to throw can be a good thing for your team!

DODGEBALLISM: *"BALL CONTROL"* - the concept of actively managing the number of balls your team controls at any given time throughout the game so you are never at a large disadvantage.

DODGEBALLISM: *"REBOUNDS"* - thrown balls that miss their targets and bounce off the wall behind them.

Catching People Off Guard

Situations will arise where people on the opposing team are not paying attention to you. If a player doesn't think you have a ball? Throw! If a player is spaced out? Throw at them. If a player is visually locked in on another thrower on your team? Gun them out. If two players on the other team are holding a little conference on who to throw at on your team? Throw! Another fun one can be when a player is coming onto the court after their team makes a catch. Or after a player comes back into the game after shagging a ball. People frequently let their guard down. Make them pay.

DODGEBALLISM: _"SHAGGING"_ - legally going out of bounds to retrieve a ball. This term can also apply to collecting balls in play at the back of your side of the court.

Sniping

Players are most vulnerable to being thrown at while they are throwing. This is because once they commit themselves, their throwing motion creates physical momentum that makes it difficult for them to alter their course mid-delivery. They also tend to keep their eye on the ball they just threw to see if it hits their target. So keep an eye out for opportunities to throw at players after they have started throwing. If you time it right and aim well, it's one successful snipe.

Vulnerable Targets

Immediately after throwing, players tend to be close to the line and then find themselves without a ball. Before they get a chance to run back from the line, throw at them. Throwing at a player while they are backpedaling can be really effective. Also, a player who is near the line is generally a better target than someone further back.

Throwing With Intimidation and Attitude: A Competitive Edge

A lot of people seem like they throw a lot harder than they actually do because they act like they are going to smash your face to death with the ball. If you think you can play the part, try sporting a menacing look on your face when you throw. Or a cool, calculated one. A harsh yell, grunt, or perplexing phrase ("MY TURN!"*) uttered while throwing can also distract people from catching you.

With offense, you want to be the alpha. You want to be the lion that screws everything it sees and eats all its competition. There are ways you can assert your dominance that will make you an undeniable force.

* As famously said by O.G. Extreme Dodgeball legend "Super" Dave Benedetto.

DODGECHANICS PRO TIP

ADD A LITTLE ATTITUDE TO YOUR GAME. IT WILL INCREASE THE PSYCHOLOGICAL VELOCITY OF YOUR THROWS.

Be a Leader

Coordinate your team. Lead them in silly chants on the sidelines. Point out who has balls on the other side. Yell at people when you need to. Act like you're the one in charge out there. It will make you a center of attention to the other team. More powerful. More something to be reckoned with.

Simply Throwing HARD

This is for people with rocket arms. Throwing hard itself can be intimidating to the other side. Even if you aren't targeting someone in particular. Sometimes it's good to just rail one between players on the opposing team to set them back on their heels and make them afraid. Fear equals less likely to catch.

Baiting With a Lob

Another way you can show your dominance is with a little trickery. This tactic can only be done if you have two balls. The idea is that you toss one of the balls high up in the air towards your target. This ball would be easy for your opponent to catch. Now the timing kicks in. Just before they are able to catch the ball, you drill them with the one you are holding onto. You may want to practice this a bit with a friend before you try it in a game — it's embarrassing having the lob caught.

Hiding Balls

Most people are wide enough that they can hide a ball behind their back. If someone doesn't know if you have a ball, it can make them uneasy about you as a potential threat. They may not see you at all! So if you can sneak up along the sideline with a ball hidden behind your back, you'll often times find someone on the opposing side who will not be ready for your throw when you unleash it.

Suicides

You will definitely get a reputation as someone to be feared if you are good at suiciding people. It's a highly aggressive maneuver where you jump over the center line into the opponent's side of the court (so you can close more of the distance between you and your target) and then launch a throw before your feet touch the ground.

DODGEBALLISM: *"SUICIDE"* - jumping over the center line to throw a ball (while you are still in the air) at an opponent.

Throwing From Behind Someone

More sneaky business here. People can be really tricked by a ball that seems to fly out of nowhere. You can throw from behind one of your teammates to good effect if your arm is strong enough.

No-Look Throws

Another way you can become more feared on the court is if you develop a throw that (accurately) targets a player in a different direction than where you're looking or planting your feet toward.

How to Spin Your Throws

Putting spin on your throw makes it harder to catch. One way you can accomplish this is by flicking your wrist while throwing. For example, if you throw sidearm, are right-handed and flick your wrist in a clockwise motion while throwing, the ball will have backspin. If you flick your wrist in a counter-clockwise motion, it will have top spin.

Top Spin

If you generate top spin in your throw, the ball will attempt to "run" its target over by spinning towards it. Sometimes you run the risk of a pop-up if you hit your target at a bad angle or don't throw hard enough. But a ball with top spin is definitely harder to catch.

Back Spin

Back spin on a thrown ball has the opposite affect; it tries to "retreat" from the player trying to catch it. The result is that the ball will tend to spin directly into the ground, which makes it less prone to pop-ups and subsequent catches.

Curveballs

Some players, by virtue of the way they grip the ball and throw, can toss a curveball not unlike the baseball variety. Once mastered, the curveball can drop out of nowhere and nip people in the feet. Nearly impossible to catch, too.

Knuckle Balls

Some balls, especially those that are lightweight and thin, have a tendency to "knuckle" around, meaning they will seem to randomly jerk around while heading towards their intended target. This can make them hard to catch.

**DODGECHANICS
PRO TIP**

ADDING SPINS TO YOUR THROWS CAN GIVE YOUR THROWING ARSENAL AN ENTIRE NEW DIMENSION OF EFFECTIVENESS.

Advanced Throwing Techniques

Here's a few things that might be better to try adding to your throwing arsenal after you've mastered the fundamentals. You'll notice the handy ball rating system below. One ball means it's the easiest to try, five stars means it might be very difficult.

Knowing When to Pass the Ball

 ONE BALL RATING

When it comes to advanced techniques, I like to start out with this one... because unless you are the best thrower on the court, in game-deciding situations you might simply be better off passing the ball to a teammate. I've got a strong arm, but even I realize that there are times it's best to give your best throwers the ball. If you are admittedly a terrible thrower and aren't an aggressive defender, and you have a ball in your hands, what good does it do your team if you hold onto a ball or throw it? Just think about that. Consider putting your ego aside. Get better or pass along the ball to someone who can do more damage with it.

Pinching Clinic

 ONE BALL RATING

Some leagues allow you to pinch the ball with your hand when you grip it. Others, including many rec leagues, don't. There's no denying that pinching the ball can increase your throwing power and precision. Not to mention make you a better defender because you're less likely to drop the ball you're defending yourself with.

DODGEBALLISM: _"PINCHING"_ - forcibly gripping a ball
   in such a manner where "rubber meets rubber"

If you can't legally pinch in your league, athletic tape on your main gripping fingers can help immensely in gripping the ball well. I tape my thumb, pointer, middle and ring fingers. You will tape different fingers depending on which ones you use most. For balls that are especially tough to grip, I've even taped my fingers with the sticky side out to good effect. Or you can buy a football wide receiver's glove. I've seen those work well, too, and you also get the advantage of possibly being able to catch better with them. The other solution that doesn't involve tape or gloves is to do a half pinch or a pinch that is so quick it's not detectable by a human ref.

Half Pinch   **Full Pinch**

A pinch is typically considered when "rubber meets rubber." Such as when your hand is gripped tightly into a fist while holding the ball. A half-pinch is getting some of your fingers tucked into the ball without squeezing your fist all the way together. That way you will get a lot of the benefits of a pinch without making an illegal throw. Like I was saying, you can also just try doing a real quick pinch during part of your delivery and that will fly a lot of the time. The human eye can only see so much and a lot of the time refs can't even see your grip from where they are standing, especially not while your arm is moving fast. Be forewarned, there are some leagues where you will get called out if they even suspect you are pinching, and if you're trying to sneak them it definitely puts you in a gray area when it comes to sportsmanship.

41

Forcing Players Out of Bounds

 TWO BALLS RATING

In leagues where dodging out of bounds is illegal, you can get people out by throwing at them when they are hugging the line. If they are scared or just aren't paying attention to the court boundaries, they may jump out of bounds. Easy out.

Tracking a Running Target

 THREE BALLS RATING

This is a lot like playing the old arcade game Paperboy. Or NES Duck Hunt. You have to learn how to anticipate where the target is going to be in the future while you are throwing. The key is to aim ahead of the direction they are heading. If you're throwing with other people, you don't have to worry as much about being accurate. Or you can wait for them to stop running if you want. They might be tired after they stop.

Throwing Out Great Catchers

 FIVE BALLS RATING

If you are facing a catch-o-saurus, the best offense can sometimes be to back off of them until all the other threats are gone. In the meantime, you can look for opportunities to catch them off guard and then unload on them as a team when they are the last player in. Then aim for the shoulders or feet.

Throwing From Your Knees!

 FIVE BALLS

Yeah, it sounds absurd... but give it a shot when you are playing defense. If your arm is strong enough, you can chuck a ball at someone when they least expect it while being crouched or kneeling in a defensive position. It will definitely put a lot of strain on the shoulder since you can hardly put any of your hips into it. This is a surprise move, so timing is key.

CATCHING

How to Catch

I preface this chapter by saying that catching, perhaps more than any other aspect of the game, contributes most to winning matches. Catches can create wild tempo swings in your team's favor, or the opponent's. A series of 2 or 3 catches can turn a game when you have only a player or two left into a game you end up dominating.

The Fundamentals of Catching

Commitment to the Catch

Dodging and catching can be competing mentalities. Let me explain. At some point as a player, you may struggle with deciding when is best to dodge and when is best to try and catch. One thing is for certain: if you aren't confident you can catch a ball, you most likely won't. So that's tip number one on catching: commit, and believe you can.

Track the Incoming Ball

Part of committing to catch is zeroing in on the ball. Make that ball your sole focus without putting pressure on yourself to actually make the catch. Act as if catching that ball is going to be the easiest thing in the world. So easy you don't even have to think about it. Because that's a huge part of catching... getting into a thought-free "zone" where you become a catch-o-saurus. A ball-stopping samurai.

Get Into Position

Once you're in the right mental state, it helps to execute a catch if you're in optimal catching stance. Luckily, the best dodging stance is also the best place from which to initiate a catch: knees bent, body squared against the opponent and leaning forward slightly, weight slightly on the balls of the feet, arms loose, and eyes wide open.

Catching Styles

Bread Basket Style

The "bread basket" catch is the safest way to catch most balls thrown at you. With this technique, you use your lower abdomen and arms to cradle a ball that is thrown at you. The ball can hit your chest then deflect into your arms or vice-versa. The point is that the chances are multiplied because at some point the ball is going to hit the softest part of your body and that will cushion the force of the throw. You will also have created a neat pocket using your body into which the ball (hopefully) makes a one-way entry.. I've also seen people successfully lift up a knee while catching the ball this way to increase the likelihood of a catch. The trick to bread basket catching is timing it right and framing your "pocket" to the incoming throw at the right angle. The rest is easy peasy.

It's even easier to do a breadbasket while kneeling on the than while standing up, because when you lean forward the pocket is created for you. All you have to do is get your arms underneath the ball when it comes in and suck it up into your abdomen. You can also use your knees when they are slightly apart to help cradle a ball. I've caught balls just with my knees that way.

You can also breadbasket catch when you have a ball in your hands, or better yet if you have two!

The Claw Style

When I'm not breadbasket catching, I'll sometimes try to catch stuff that is around my upper torso by doing the "claw" catch. This catch really relies on fast reflexes because if you don't time it right, you will look foolish. You wrap one arm sideways around the incoming ball and then wrap the other arm underneath the ball. When the ball is successfully caught, you will have secured it by both horizontal and vertical axis in kind of a cross shape with your arms in front of the ball.

Hands Catching

Hands catching is also totally possible. The trick with catching a ball with your hands alone is to avoid injuring your fingers. A technique taught to me by one of the best hand catchers I've ever seen is to catch the ball like a soccer goalie: put your spread-open hands (palms facing out) towards the opposition, then line up the tips of your thumbs and index fingers. It'll look kinda like a spade or diamond depending on the shape of your hands. Then you just frame up the incoming ball with your hands and let your hands fall around the sides of it, cushioning the ball as it comes in towards your body.

Arm Traps

You can also catch a ball with one arm by trapping the ball with your arm and body. One of the most common ways I've done this is by acting almost like I'm a running back carrying a football. The triangle shape you create with your arm against your body is the cradle with which you can catch the ball with.

Advanced Catching Techniques

Once you've mastered the basics of catching, try moving on to these more advanced strategies. The ball rating system below visually demonstrates the difficulty level, from one being the easiest to five being the most challenging.

Know Who the Weak Throwers Are

 ONE BALL RATING

Identify the weak throwers on the other team and get into position to catch them when they throw. You'll know when you've got someone on the other side who's a guaranteed catch every time. Use that info to your advantage.

Baiting Throwers

 ONE BALL RATING

Baiting throwers into targeting you can be a lot of fun. It's easy. Just pretend like you don't see someone with a ball. Then as soon as they start throwing at you, get mentally prepared to catch. They'll be saying, "Hello, out line."

Drop and Catch

 THREE BALL RATING

The "drop and catch" is the next best way to bait throwers into tossing catchable balls at you. You do this by pretending like you are going to block their throw with your ball, then the second they release the ball, you drop your ball off to the side and prepare to catch their ball. It's magic when you pull it off.

49

Deflect Missed Catches

 THREE BALL RATING

When catching, you can often deflect a missed catch into the air for someone else on your team to catch. They will save you and the catch still counts in most leagues, so it's a win-win for you. So if you sense you don't have a handle on an incoming ball, over time you will learn to bounce it up or in another direction.

Egg Them On

 FOUR BALL RATING

You can also bait throwers simply by standing in the middle of the court or close towards the center line without a ball. You have to be careful though; this can be viewed as cockiness. And I know when someone tries this against me the gut instinct is to throw as hard at them as humanly possible to make them pay for their disrespect of my arm.

Catch the Bait

 FIVE BALL RATING

You will sometimes have the chance to catch a "bait lob." A bait lob is when someone on the other side with a really good arm tries to bait you into catching an underhanded toss when they have a second ball ready to blast you with. If you time it right, you can catch the bait lob and dodge the second ball they throw at you. It's hilarious when it happens. Sometimes you get blasted pretty good trying though. I find it's like 50/50 chances when I try.

DODGING

Basic Dodging Strategy

Court Awareness

Yes, dodging is an art of avoidance... but more one of awareness. The best tip I can give you is to start thinking about how you can avoid being thrown at in the first place.

Peripheral vision is key. You need to start scanning for where the balls are on the other side so you are aware of who could throw at you. Some people will pretend like they have a ball. It's kinda like that old shell game. You usually get a chance to see who has a ball before people hide them. Remember who has them so you are prepared.

Know Your Opponent

Learn the tendencies of the throwers on the other side. How long does it take for their wind-up? Does their throw come straight at you, or does it curve down? Do they throw indiscriminately? This information will help you assess what to do when they pick you as a target.

Always Face the Front

Never turn your back to the other team. Never ever ever EVER! No better way to paint a target on your back than this.

Avoid Where the Balls Are on the Other Side

Move away from the side of the court where all the throwers are lining up to throw at your team.

The Back Left Corner Advantage

Put yourself in the back left corner (from your perspective), generally the least-thrown-at part of the court. This is because most throwers are right-handed and it's easier for them to follow through all the way when they throw towards their left.

Actually, either side of the court is preferable to being somewhere in the middle when dodging. This is because it's easier to scan the court when you don't have to worry about balls coming at you from a wider range of angles.

Find Cover

Get behind someone. Preferably someone with a ball who knows how to block with it. Next best, you could get behind someone who won't jump out of the way if a ball comes. Like Malcolm. Or someone who's a great catcher. As a last resort, you could get behind an "easy out" who couldn't get out of the way in time if they tried. It could save your hide, but could also be a real jerk move. And I don't recommend pulling those kinds of stunts frequently. Gives you a bad rep on and off the court.

Keep Your Distance

Get as far back from the center line as you can. More distance equals more reaction time when someone throws at you. And the ball will lose speed over long distances.

Pick a Dodging Direction

Generally, the best way to dodge a right-handed thrower is to dodge to your left, the best way to dodge a left-handed thrower is to dodge to your right. So be ready. When they are halfway in their windup is the time to start executing your dodge, preferably right before they are releasing the ball. It's impossible at that time for a thrower to change where they are sending it. So they'll have to anticipate your dodge in order to hit you.

Personal Ball Control

Keeping a ball in your hands is a strong deterrent to throwers. If you have a ball you can pump fake, get up to the center line to keep them away from it, and defend yourself really well by blocking.

Use the Sidelines

Being aware of the sidelines can be helpful. If you hunker down against one of the sidelines, it basically eliminates a lot of the angles the opposition can throw at you from and makes it really hard for them to hit you on one side of your body.

Timely Shagging

Shagging balls can rule. No, this is not humping the ball. "Shagging" here means going out of bounds to retrieve a ball, and it's common slang on the court. If your league allows you to shag balls out of bounds, there will be times when you can legally run out of bounds to shag a ball as the other team's throwers are launching balls at you. Do it.

Stay on Your Toes

Keep your feet light and your legs bouncy, ready to move quickly in any direction as needed. When combined with court awareness, you will be ready to quickly assess and react to incoming threats.

Intimidation Defense

It's the same advice you'd get about walking down a dark alley at night. Don't look like a target. Even if you can't catch to save your life, assume a supremely confident catching stance. Square your body to the opposition, have your knees loosely bent, lean on the balls of your feet a little, have your arms open wide. You will look like you're definitely prepared for their throw should they choose to aim at you.

Stare Them Down

Look throwers straight in the eyes. Looking menacing can also help. Being scared is another great way to paint a bulls-eye on yourself. So don't be afraid. Also, throwers tend to want to throw at people who are not prepared for the throw. So by making eye contact you let them know that you are aware of them. That you may be completely prepared for what they have in store.

Defensive Pump Faking

Pump-faking when you have a ball is a great way to keep the other team's throwers on edge and away from you. It's most effective right before someone tries to throw or even during their motion. The thing throwers hate worst of all is to see someone throwing at them while they are launching away. It takes their attention away and their throw will suffer for it.

Now, there are two important keys to this strategy. First, you absolutely have to unload on your opponent at least once every twenty times or so that you pump fake. Otherwise, they'll just know you never throw the ball and it won't scare them. The other thing… your pump fakes need to be sold really well! You have to have the same aggression on your face when you pump fake that you have when you throw. The only difference is that you don't actually release the ball. You can also pump fake from more of an upright stance as if you're going to do a quick lob throw down at their feet. Same rules apply for that as well in terms of actually throwing every once in awhile and really selling every fake throw.

Point Them Out

Pointing at people on the other side who have balls and calling them out ("Hey, watch out for left side!") can be a good way to disarm them in a sense. If you make it clear you know they have a ball, it makes you a harder target in their mind. Plus this helps your teammates avoid being caught off-guard.

Pretend You Have a Ball

I will often pretend that I have a ball. Confidently standing with my arm behind my back, I can keep a lot of throwers away from the line and away from me. You can pump-fake as well even if you don't have a ball. Believe me, it works! Although it's obviously less effective after everyone on the other side realizes you don't really have a ball.

YELL!

Yelling just about anything and timing it correctly can throw the opposing team off. It's a great distraction technique, and if you do it repeatedly it can grate on the other side throughout a game. I like doing it right as throwers are beginning their throwing motion. Something like "Hey!" or "Watch out!" works well.

Dodging Mechanics

Controlling Your Body with Flexibility

The simplest dodging skill to master is contorting your body to avoid throws. It's possible to dodge most high throws without actually taking a step in any direction. The way you do this is by twisting your torso, turning your body sideways, bending over, bending sideways, bending backwards... lots of bending. If you're not a yogi, I would suggest easing your way into this. Yoga will help you refine this technique.

Quick Directional Bursts

Changing directions quickly makes you a difficult target to lock in on. So right before someone throws at you, try starting to move a couple of steps in one direction, then completely change direction as they throw at you.

Strafe to Safety

If you aren't a great Subway sandwich artist, then your skill at strafing (moving sideways) may be less than average. Fortunately you can learn how to move your body from side to side. If you are in the correct dodging position, strafing becomes an easy bouncing motion from putting all your weight on one side to the other. You can start to jump a bit that way, and before you know it, you can start taking steps sideways to avoid balls thrown at you. The ultimate way to develop this is by running up stadium stairs sideways, rotating one leg in front of the other.

Learn to Leap

Since throwers tend to aim for the legs a lot, try learning how to jump over low throws. The best way is to tuck your legs under you or behind you when you jump. Sometimes you can't avoid it, but just try not to jump over a ball when there is someone behind you. They will not be happy if the ball you jump to avoid hits them instead.

A great exercise to do for this is jumping up onto a high platform repeatedly.

Forwards and Backwards

Vertical movement (like running forward and backpedaling) can save you on the court. The first thing I recommend learning is how to backpedal quickly after throwing a ball. The reason this is important is because during your throw and immediately after your throw are the times that you are most vulnerable to being thrown at. Another pro trick you'll pick up is to hop forward or backwards to avoid a ball thrown at you that's coming in at an angle.

Remember that if you jump backwards it increases the likelihood that a ball thrown low to the ground hits the ground before it hits you.

Make Your Getaway

There are some cases (like when multiple balls are about to be thrown at you) when running across the back of the court is effective. The key is initiating your getaway from one side of the court to the other before their throwers get a chance to target you and start their throws. That's because decent throwers can track a running target. Especially when they are operating in a pack. So get running before you're a murdered Milly!

Get Low

One trick that regularly keeps me alive on the court is to get as low to the ground as I can... as fast as I can. If you know someone is about to throw at you, try going from standing up to lying belly-down on the ground in an instant. If you time it right (mid-throw), the thrower will not be able to control the ball sufficiently to hit you. Just keep in mind that while you are prone you are a very easy target.

DRILL SERGEANT SAYS:

STAND IN THE BACK RIGHT CORNER OF THE COURT. STRAFE LEFT FROM ONE SIDE OF THE COURT TO THE OTHER, THEN STRAFE RIGHT ALL THE WAY BACK. THEN RUN FORWARD TO THE CENTER LINE. THEN BACKPEDAL ALL THE WAY BACK TO THE BACK LINE. THEN PRACTICE RUNNING FULL SPEED ACROSS THE COURT AS IF YOU WERE AVOIDING THROWS. DO THIS IN EACH DIRECTION. REPEAT THE ENTIRE DRILL A COUPLE TIMES AND IDENTIFY WHERE YOU ARE THE WEAKEST SO THAT YOU CAN STRENGTHEN THAT ASPECT OF YOUR AGILITY.

Defensive Styles and Stances

The Crouch

The dodgeball defense diet consists of at least two to three servings of crouching per game. You can easily crouch to dodge a ball thrown at your chest or head. Or simply do it to make yourself a harder target to aim at. You can also crouch in preparation to a Super Mario jump up high in the air (upward punch into imaginary question mark block optional). Crouching while you have a ball is the ultimate defensive position to find yourself in. So crouching good.

Kneeling

Kneeling is taking crouching even lower to the ground and putting your knees flat on the ground and tucking or untucking your feet. If I tuck my feet in behind my butt and sit on my legs, it makes me the smallest possible target when I fold my upper body over my legs and put my hands over my head for protection. Sometimes that's all you can do (and pray) if you don't have a ball to protect yourself with. Kneeling is also a great position to defend yourself with when you have a ball. It's also an even better position to try and catch from than crouching. Although pro players who are crouching can still quickly splay their knees to the ground and be in kneeling position in time to make a catch if necessary. I just find it easier to be in catching position all the time sometimes. Just remember to tuck your feet in behind you, because sometimes your feet can get nicked by a ball if you aren't careful.

Sliding on your knees after running to dodge stuff can be fun, especially when you have a ball. Just make sure you have knee pads on!

Getting Small Quickly

This is all about curling up into a ball. Sitting on your knees and bringing your forehead down towards the floor. Put your hands over your head. If you can turtle like this and do it quickly, it's a great way to dodge a throw. Just be careful: you'll need to get back up quickly to reassess after the wave of throws misses you.

DODGECHANICS PRO TIP

WHEN JUMPING OVER OR CONTORTING AROUND
A THROW AREN'T GOOD OPTIONS, GETTING
SMALL AND LOW TO THE GROUND
(AND DOING IT QUICKLY)
CAN BE A VERY EFFECTIVE WAY TO DODGE.

Advanced Dodging Strategy

Take a Roll

 THREE BALLS

I've also rolled around on occasion to avoid throws. This is a little more risky since it's about as effective to just get small and strafe sideways, and you won't have to take your eyes off the throwers if you strafe. It's not possible to make a catch while you're rolling. Or damned near impossible. So that's another drawback.

Assessing Multiple Threats

 FIVE BALLS

A high-level tactic to acquire is dodging multiple balls at once. If you don't have a ball in your hands, this can be damned near impossible. Obviously, the less skilled the throwers, and the fewer the balls coming at you at once, the easier it is to dodge them. I will say this: Quickly moving in unexpected direction the moment before your opponents' balls leave their hands gives you the best chance. For example, you sell it like you are going to run to the right across the court, then the moment they throw, you totally change directions and leap to the left. Another thing that I've found that works sometimes is quickly make yourself as small as humanly possible in a ball on the ground, say a prayer (while covering your head), and basically duck all the throws if you're lucky. You can also try faking that you are going to throw as they are throwing and that may scare a couple of your opponents who were planning to throw from throwing. That momentarily reducing the number of throwers on the other side helps even the odds in your favor!

BLOCKING

How to Block

Blocking Technique

You gotta first learn how to correctly block using a ball. The best way most of the time is with two hands. You want to cross your thumbs, and form a "butterfly" with your hands behind the ball, gripping the ball with your fingers without putting your fingers across the front of the ball. This gives you a good surface from which to block cleanly with.

You want to hold the ball out far enough from your body that if you block it into the ground it won't hit your feet or lower body. Aim the clean surface of your blocking ball exactly at the incoming thrown ball to block the ball directly back at the thrower. Aim it slightly above the incoming thrown ball to deflect it downward. Aim it slightly below the incoming ball to deflect it into the air.

Deflecting the ball precisely takes a lot of practice. You will get yourself out a lot by deflecting into your feet or up into your noggin until you master the technique. Some throws are going to have unpredictable spin on them that make them virtually impossible to safely block any way but squarely.

Bear Swipe

Another great one is doing the Bear Swipe. You literally bat an incoming ball out of the way using a ball you are holding with one hand. Once again, having a very strong grip on the ball is required or you will drop the ball. Most leagues will call you out for that even if the thrown ball doesn't hit you.

Basketball Pass

Here's a fun blocking technique that I think is kinda unfair it's so effective. When a ball is incoming, just basketball pass your ball into the incoming ball. Most leagues count a ball that hits another ball as dead, so even if the ball is really close to you when you throw, you'll be safe.

Block Jump

Blocking + jumping can almost make you an invincible target. Practice jumping in the air while holding the ball in front of you.

Blocking Responsibilities

When you have a ball in your hands, it is the ultimate defensive tool. For this reason, if you aren't going to throw the ball immediately, it's your job to see how you can help defend your team with it. Blocking for yourself and others is a key skill to master.

Do not block balls sideways into your teammates. They will hate you for it. Also, don't jump in the air while blocking when people are behind you. They will also hate you for that and you will have to buy them drinks. Unless you communicate to them what you are planning to do ahead of time.

Mastering the Deflection

A lot of leagues will reward players who catch deflections. Blocking a thrown ball so that a teammate catches it is a great way to contribute. There are two things to remember here.

First, you have the best chance of blocking a ball into the air if you aim your ball underneath the thrown ball, or intentionally "bat" the ball into the air using your ball.

Second, make sure to angle your chest so you are leaning backwards. That way if the ball does hit your chest, it will be more likely to pop up into the air and be caught.

DODGEBALLISM: *"DEFLECTION"* - a live ball that has been blocked by a ball or has hit a player but still hasn't hit a wall or the floor.

DRILL SERGEANT SAYS:

TOSS A BALL AROUND WITH A FRIEND. YOU ARE NOT ALLOWED TO CATCH THE BALL. YOU CAN ONLY DEFLECT IT OFF YOUR CHEST OR BAT IT UP WITH YOUR ARMS OR HANDS. THIS WAY, YOU WILL SLOWLY MASTER THE SKILL OF BATTING A BALL IN THE AIR WITH YOUR BODY AND CATCHING IT.

WHAT TYPE OF PLAYER ARE YOU?

SOON AFTER YOU START PLAYING, you will discover that you have a unique set of talents. Your skills will make you best suited for a certain kind of role on your team. Here are the different player types and how they typically help out. Many people are combinations of these player types.

DODGECHANICS PRO TIP

FIGURING OUT WHAT TYPE OF PLAYER YOU ARE HELPS YOU TO FIT INTO A TEAM DYNAMIC.

On-Court General

You lead by example and help coordinate attack and defense. You keep track of ball control. You get your best throwers paired up. You point out when people have a ball, or that they are faking like they do. You are an energy drink in human form and your team feeds off you.

Things to watch out for:
- Being too bossy
- Giving bad information
- Making bad/rash decisions

Hard Thrower

People on the other side can't catch you. They generally flinch when you start throwing.

Things to watch out for:
- Throwing alone against a good catcher
- Getting sniped while throwing
- Acting like a douchebag just because you can throw hard

Intimidator

Whether you have a strong arm or not, you are one mean motherfucker on the court. People are generally intimidated by your presence. You command the attention of the other side through your combination of skill and swagger.

Things to watch out for:
- Coming across as too cocky
- Not having the goods to deliver upon your threatening nature
- Lay back every once in awhile. It helps to not be noticed sometimes.

Gunslinger

You live on the wild side, and constantly take chances to gun people out. You'll throw when you aren't supposed to and put yourself in dangerous situations often. You throw sometimes just because you want to, not necessarily because it will really help your team.

Things to watch out for:
- Your teammates hating your ass for not being a team player
- Not having the skills to stay in the game long with risky play
- Getting caught because you prolly throw alone a lot

Line Player

You like to get up to the center line with a ball and keep the opposition far back. You usually do this with a bunch of pump faking and other aggressive posturing. Every once in awhile, you'll try to snipe someone cross-court or nail someone nearby in the foot.

Things to watch out for:
- Getting sniped in the foot yourself when you are in close range
- Holding onto the ball too much and then people not taking you seriously
- Getting pushed back too frequently from the center line instead of holding it

Defender

You are the last person the other side wants to have to get out at the end of a game. You are a scrapper and survivor out there. You are a good dodger, deflector, and probably can catch well, too. You don't throw much and rely on your defensive game to contribute. At the end of games you try to spark a rally by getting a catch to bring in teammates.

Things to watch out for:
- If you can't catch well, it won't help much to survive until the end
- Being too passive when it comes to offense, missing key opportunities
- Playing selfishly as you are surviving

Court Jester

You are out there primarily to distract the other team. You dance around, wave your hands in the air, basically playing like a rodeo clown. You kill the other team with annoyance and/or charm.

Things to watch out for:
- The need for extremely vigilant court awareness
- Being so unskilled that you are an automatic out
- Being a distraction to your own team

Acrobat

You like to jump around a lot. You use spin throws or other out-there maneuvers to make up for a less-than-scary skill set. You have tricks up your sleeve. You often draw the fire of the opponent because you need space up in front of your team to operate your wild gymnastics.

Things to watch out for:

- Being too predictable in your movements to avoid being an easy out
- Playing erratically (with no strategy) or apart from your team
- Using your on-court antics as an excuse for not developing your game

Sniper

The sniper watches for opportunities to catch people on the other side off guard and then throws at them. Their aim is usually really good.

Things to watch out for:

- Giving up ball control at a critical time in the game
- Being sure your target isn't baiting you into throwing at them
- Making sure you are safe to throw yourself

Loudmouth

You yell a lot at your teammates, the refs, and the other side. You are constantly barking out commands, pointing out who has balls on the other side, and managing your team's obligation to yield ball control.

Things to watch out for:
- Your safety in the parking lot after the games for mouthing off too much
- Your teammates tuning you out or taking your yelling personally
- Your focus on being loud taking precedence over playing the game

Jack of All Trades

The Jack of All Trades has a well-rounded skill set and no glaring weaknesses.

They can often be stars on a team by virtue of their versatility.

Things to watch out for:
- Knowing how to use which skill at which appropriate time
- Continue developing skills - might possibly be the best thrower out there someday!
- May not fit into typical team strategy roles because of adaptive skill set. Captain will need to know how to best utilize you.

Countdowner

The countdown leader coordinates throwers who are throwing together. They execute a count-down that everyone agrees to, and that helps the throwers throw together at the same time.

Things to watch out for:
- Initiating your countdown before all the throwers are ready
- Getting distracted by leading a countdown and getting sniped
- Executing the countdown in a way that makes sense to all the throwers

Survivalist

The Survivalist is like the guy they drop in Siberia with nothing but a compass and a knife. He can dodge, scrap it out, and survive until the end of almost any game.

Things to watch out for:
- Your egotistical instinct to survive getting in the way of what's best for the team. There will be times when it's better for you to sacrifice staying in the game so your team has a better chance of winning.
- Perhaps less willingness to catch because you don't want to risk possibly getting out (Hone those catching skills so you can become a hybrid with the Catch-o-saurus.)
- Might occasionally mistake a teammate for a wild bear from time to time

Catch-o-saurus

People try not to throw at you because it seems like you catch almost everything. You probably default to being primarily a catcher because you can't throw or because you can't throw.

Things to watch out for:
- Not being a good catcher anywhere but your breadbasket
- Multiple people throwing at you at once
- Trying to catch balls even you shouldn't attempt

Shagger

In some leagues, they let you have a ball shagger on the side of the court opposite the outline. The shagger plays the important role of shagging balls after they are out.

Often a less physically gifted player will take this position, though no one should feel above this important task. They go up close to the center line and stay aware of incoming balls they may be able to shag for their team.

Things to watch out for:
- Not paying attention and missing opportunities to shag balls for your team
- Accidentally getting hit by a thrower on the other side who thinks you are still in the game
- Resigning yourself to sitting out the rest of the game instead of getting back in there and improving your skills

TEAM STRATEGY

Assembling Your Team

If you are crafting a team for a tournament or league, it's important to know a few things first:

1. What's the competition level of the league or tournament?
2. How big is your team?
3. Is there a male:female ratio requirement?
4. Can you easily get good subs for the team if someone can't make it?
5. What kind of players do I need on my team?

Competition Level Affecting Team Composition

If you're playing in a rec league where the motto is "Don't Be A Jerk" or something similar, you've got to be mindful of how stacking your team could negatively impact the fun culture the league is trying to establish. Unless you actually are a jerk, and like beating up on people just trying to have a good time. I hope not!

When playing in a competitive league, EVERY roster spot should make an impact and almost every team needs at least a couple real ringers. That's right, no dead weight + ringers with rocket arms is what you want. You are also going to want great catchers on your team, and a captain who knows what they are talking about. The captain should have a strategy in mind when assembling the roster, and add players who are down to execute that plan.

If you've got a brand new team that's never played dodgeball before, unless you're masochistic try finding a relatively chill league to start out in. In the past I've seen corporate teams join competitive leagues and just get trashed twelve to nothing every week and that's no fun for anyone... Surprisingly not even the teams that beat them!

If you have any questions about what the competition level is of a league, you can flat out just ask the manager of the league, or check out their games. It's good to do your homework with this ahead of time.

Team Size Affecting Team Composition

The smaller the team, the more important every player on that team is and the more dialed in the team strategy needs to be. In competitive leagues with 6 or fewer players on a team, there's no room for players that don't make an impact.

Male:Female Ratio Affecting Team Composition

Co-ed leagues typically have rules in place that penalize teams that can't show up with a minimum number of females on the court. So when creating a co-ed team, it's good practice to bring female players on board who can reliably show up to the games. And have a handful of potential subs in mind for those weeks where people make other plans or get sick.

Ability to Get Subs Easily

In competitive leagues, you never want to be short players - unless the best available sub doesn't add much of anything. Sometimes being a player or two short is actually an advantage if you have no dead weight on your squad. This is in part because your out line will be full of impact players ready to come back into the game on a catch.

If you need a sub for one of your ringers, it's best to find another ringer who fits into your team strategy. Otherwise you might be missing the talent and spark your regular ringer brings week in week out.

Typical Team Composition

Unless the league has very small rosters of 6 or less, you usually will want a mix of different types of players:

1. A couple of vocal leaders who help relay the team strategy on the court as the game is happening. One of them should probably be the captain.
2. At least a couple deadly throwers, but more if you can find them.
3. A couple of players who do a great job of holding the line and the corners. They don't mind holding onto a ball and protecting your throwers.
4. A few players who are awesome catchers. You can never have enough stellar catchers.
5. A couple players who are good at "surviving" out there. These are players who by themselves can rally the team with a catch, or drag out a game enough at the end to earn a win.

Basic Team Strategy

If you are a captain, now that you have your team all ready to roll, how are you planning to win games with them? Even if you don't care much about winning, all it takes is a little effort to get a solid strategy in place that will greatly reduce your chances of getting blown out. Here are some tactics worth investing in as a team.

When on Offense...

Ball Control

Probably the worst team mistake is having no concept of how to maintain ball control. Ball control is when you have more balls than the other side has. This is the best position to be in because you can then confidently go on offense and still retain enough balls to protect your throwers and have a couple left to defend your team with should you lose ball control during your attack wave. Bad teams tend to get eager beaver and throw all the balls over to the other side, painting big red circle targets on themselves.

Usually leagues have rules that govern ball control, dictating that the team with ball control has a limited amount of time to throw until they no longer have ball control.

A conservative team throwing strategy is typically employed in competitive leagues so that teams only throw enough balls to barely surrender ball control. For example, if your game has seven balls and you are in possession of four of them, you would want to throw one or maybe two of those balls at the most. That's because you'll want to have a couple of people left with balls to protect your throwers, and then play defense along the sides afterwards.

DODGECHANICS PRO TIP

BALL CONTROL MANAGEMENT IS PERHAPS THE MOST IMPORTANT TEAM SKILL TO MASTER.

Throw Together

Catching a single throw seems like a breeze compared to facing multiple balls flying your way. That's because you don't have to decide which ball to track and catch when only one thrower is involved. Same goes for dodging; you have to process more than one bogey. Now that you understand why it's tough to be on the receiving end of more than one ball, why would you want it any other way when you are throwing? Throwing alone greatly increases your chances of getting caught or being dodged. It can be tempting sometimes to think you can gun someone out, and that may be true. Hell, sometimes I'll feel like changing the direction of my throw even when I'm about to throw with someone. I'll say through years of trial and error, in the long run, throwing with a partner will result in many more successful throws and keep you in the game longer. And your teammates won't give you the stink eye when you selfishly throw alone and get caught.

Share a Countdown

Counting down is the art of timing it so that you and your throwing partner(s) throw together at the same time. You can go a couple different ways with this. Here's one popular way. Imagine this: "3, 2, 1... THROW!" Another one is "3, 2, THROW!" And then there's the clever "1, 2, DIE!" Just make sure everyone knows when to actually throw.

One thing to keep in mind is that no matter how clear you are about when to throw during the countdown, you are still going to have slowpokes who miss the cue or crackheads who jump the gun on ya. Just do whatever you need to do to adjust your throw to match theirs. It's really important that your throw and theirs be pretty close together as far as timing goes.

Common Target

If you are bothering to throw with someone and share a countdown, why not take the extra effort and figure out who you're going to throw at together? While throwing together at different targets is better than throwing alone, throwing together at the same target beats the shit out of that.

Create a Custom Targeting Language

On targeting, if you want to quickly go after the second person from the left on the other side, you can tell your throwing partner "Two." The fourth from the left? "Four." And so on. You could also try "R2," which would be second person from the right, "L1," person farthest to the left, etc. Coming up with a quick numbering system will prevent you from having to talk about your target too much, aka "No, not that guy with the blue shirt, the other one…"

DODGECHANICS PRO TIP

USE A CUSTOM TEAM LANGUAGE TO QUICKLY COORDINATE TARGETING SPECIFIC PLAYERS ON THE OTHER SIDE.

Plan in Advance

Planning your throw well in advance can be helpful too. You can talk to your throwing buddy about who to throw at AHEAD of time. For example, if you and a throwing partner have balls, and your desired target has a ball, you could say "Immediately after Dickface McGee over there throws, let's get him." Then you will have your target already picked out and be ready to assault. Don't forget to cover your mouth with your ball while you are talking to your throwing buddy. That way you won't telegraph your throw to the other team.

Attacking At Angles

It's easier to catch or dodge a ball that's thrown from directly ahead of you than it is to catch one thrown at an angle from where you're facing. So when throwing, try not to stand directly in front of your target if you can help it, and especially not when throwing in pairs or more. You will realize amazing results when you start spacing your throwing buddies out with you on the court and attacking the same target from different angles. They will shit themselves.

Protect Your Throwers

Teams that don't protect their throwers lose all their good throwers early in the game and then get mauled 'cause they've got about as much firepower left as Pee Wee Herman. If you have a ball and aren't throwing, it's your job to help keep people on your team who are throwing safe from harm. It helps if you stand behind your throwing teammate or off to the side and pump fake at anyone who looks like they might be trying to land a snipe in on your teammate.

Fast Countering

You want to be as close to your prey as possible when throwing. The best chance to get close and have the added bonus of catching your target in a vulnerable position is right after they have thrown. Your team's mentality should be to immediately attack after their throwers finish. You will catch them at a close distance, they will be backpedaling, and then you can depants them.

DODGEBALLISM: *"FAST COUNTERS"* - throwing aggressively at an opponent immediately after they throw and are usually most vulnerable to attack.

Kill Lists

You'll notice on every team (except for really shitty ones) there are players you want to get out of the game as fast as possible. While it's desirable to immediately dispose of them, you want to be smart about it. It doesn't help as much to get them out first, because then they will be the first player back in if a catch is made by them. So... that's where a "kill list" comes in. You pick out their best players, then you kill those players in order after first taking out a few of their new or unskilled players. Then if they get a catch, they won't bring back in anyone who can immediately give them a big boost.

DODGEBALLISM. *"KILL LIST"* - a list of players you want to get out on the other team, usually ordered by the skill of the player (most skilled to least).

Passing Balls to Throwers

You can file this tip under "sometimes questionable" because the whole point of dodgeball is to have fun. If you want to win badly or your league is really competitive, it can help to have your weaker throwers pass balls over to your best throwers (or defenders). Wish it weren't true, but it sadly makes a huge difference if your worst thrower has a ball vs. your best player. The worst thrower throws a catch. The best player gets three people out in one throw. The worst thrower stands back and lets their teammates get sniped. The best player defends teammates and keeps the entire opposing team on guard. Don't force someone to give up their ball, but if they really suck you might have no choice if you want to win.

When on Defense...

Line Players: Holding the Sides

On defense, you have to have a couple of players who are aggressive at the extreme left and right sides of the court. They must remain close to the center line and do their best to keep the opposing team from coming up to throw. Eventually, it will be smart for your line players to retreat back to a turtling defensive position, but I've had games where I've been so aggressive at the line that all the throwers go to the other side. Then my team knew where all the throws were coming from, and I could snipe at their throwers easily from my side of the court.

The Quick Lob

When playing the line, executing a quick snipe against a target maybe ten or fifteen feet ahead of you is something that will strike fear into your opponent. The idea is you pump fake the hell out the other times. Maybe twenty times really sell the pump fake hard... so much so that your motion is exactly the same as it is when you actually throw. Then casually stand tall with the ball held high. Bring your arm up, pump fake a couple more times. Look at the opposing player carefully. Watch out for the perfect time when they aren't looking. Maybe they glance to the other side of the court or start pump faking. Strike like a snake. You can practice this against a wall.

DRILL SERGEANT SAYS:

STAND FIVE FEET AWAY FROM A WALL. TARGET AS LOW ON THE WALL AS POSSIBLE WITHOUT HITTING THE FLOOR. THROW THERE TEN TIMES AND THEN TAKE A STEP BACK. THROW THERE TEN MORE TIMES AND THEN TAKE ANOTHER STEP BACK. REPEAT THE THROWING DRILL UNTIL YOU'RE FIFTEEN FEET OUT AND THEN WORK BACK IN. EMPHASIS ON A QUICK RELEASE!

Stopping Rebounds

If you are standing in front of a wall, it's likely that a lot of the balls thrown at you will rebound off the wall and return to the other side before you can snag them safely. But it's very hard to stop the momentum of a team that has ball control when they keep getting it back over and over. So you have to have a team mentality of trying to stop rebounds before they go to the other side.

Three tactics are key here: not standing too close to the wall, using your hands down by your sides near the ground to try and guess where rebounds may be traveling through so you can stop them, and protecting your teammates when they try to get to a ball that is close to going over to the other side.

Calling Out Snipers and Sneaks

Intel wins both wars and kid games. Having at least a couple of players on your team acting as lookouts can be really helpful. It's simple. If you see someone trying to hide a ball who's standing on the left side waiting to snipe, call them out to your team. Yell, "Watch left!" If you see someone hiding a ball on the right side, yell, "Right side is hiding a ball!"

Spacing Out Your Team

Einstein theorized that the larger the mass of your team concentrated in one area of the court, the more likely it is your team will lose. Unless someone has a ball and you can hide behind them, there's no reason to stand anywhere close to your teammates. Spacing out your team evenly increases the chance that your team will catch all the easy grabs and be in position to react to deflected balls in time.

Pump-Faking

I've played on teams where we made it a team policy that everyone had to pump-fake throughout the game, even when we didn't have ball control or even close to it. It works. Keep the other team on edge. Don't let them feel secure while they're throwing. And when they're defending, it will be even harder for them to tell where the balls are coming from when you're also throwing.

Turtling

When you have no other choice but to retreat from the center line in the face of an incoming attack, the players on your team who have balls should fall back to defensive positions. Turtling is the art of having one player in the front holding a ball (usually crouched or knees to the ground), and then having teammates hide behind them in a single-file line. This makes it almost impossible to get people out when a highly skilled defender is in front holding a ball. You just have to watch out for throws coming in at an angle if you are in the back of a turtling situation.

Broadcast Pop-Ups

Your team should be on the lookout for pop-ups and other deflected balls. Catching them will keep one of your teammates from being out, and bring another one of them back in the game. So catches are critical. That's why if someone on your team sees a pop-up, it's their job if they can't catch it themselves to point their finger at it and yell "Pop-up!" or "Catch that!"

Situational Team Strategy

Now that we have offense and defense covered, here are some more situational tactics you can employ to be a better team.

During the Opening Rush

When the whistle blows, you don't want to be caught with your pants down. A bad start to the game can set your team back.

Assigning Runners

Your fastest players should be running for the balls. It helps to line yourself across from someone you're pretty sure you can beat to the center line.

DODGEBALLISM: *"RUNNERS"* - the players on your team who typically run for balls on the center line during the opening rush.

Going for All the Balls

If your league lets you get all the balls, try! If your league only lets you get the balls on one side of the court, see if you can get to yours really quickly... in time to scare the other team away from taking all of their balls.

Passing Balls Back to Throwers

Something that can be fun is having one of your runners, during the opening rush, toss a ball back behind the attack line to one of your team's best throwers. Doing this fast enough (and accurately to make it useful to the thrower in time) can be a challenging task, but it can definitely give your team an early advantage when executed right.

Initial Throwing Waves

The first few throwing waves are fun. Everyone's all packed together and there's nowhere to run. It's like shooting fish in a barrel. During this phase of the game, if you are a hard thrower, it's just as effective to blindly throw into the crowd as it is to target someone individually. You'll get all kinds of crazy ricochets and lots of outs.

DODGEBALLISM: *"ATTACK LINE"* - the line you must cross behind before you are allowed to throw a ball during the opening rush.

Middle Game Strategy

In the middle of the game, you typically want to establish ball control as much as possible, to make sure to always keep two balls (for line players to hold the sides), and to turtle on the left and right sides when you are on defense. Middle game is also the time it is most effective to start targeting the best players on the other side because there will be enough players in their outline to make it unlikely they will be caught back in.

DODGEBALLISM: *"TURTLING"* - crouching down in a corner with a ball in a defensive posture. Can also be used to describe a defensive team strategy where you are all hunkering down for the worst and playing very conservatively.

Finishing Off a Team

When they've just got a handful of players left, it's CRITICAL not to let the other team get a catch. I've seen countless games totally reversed by catching. When you're trying to finish off the opposition, target individual players, throw together, throw low, etc., and you will be fine. When there are fewer than five players left in the game, I recommend getting the weakest players out first and then working from there. It's likely they will have at least a couple of players you will need to focus all your attention on to get out.

Also, another key strategy during the end game is, if you have a strong player advantage, to just slow things down. Deliberately set up your throws and eliminate the final players on the other side.

Dynamic Duo Strategies

If it's just you and one other person on your team left in the game on your side, it's important to have each other's backs. I would recommend that when you are on offense, you spread out, and that the best thrower throws while the other fakes. When the other team targets your partner, try to snipe them or at least pump fake while they're throwing to help your pal survive. If one of you is a great blocker, you can also have the other player turtle up behind them on defense.

Endgame Defense

If things haven't gone well for your team and it's down to you and a few others, it's time to get smart about staying alive out there. First, look out for opportunities to make catches. If they have a weaker thrower, try to bait that person into throwing at you. Use all your dodging techniques and don't be afraid to turtle up behind someone. Remember, you've got to survive long enough to take out enough of their players to even the score, or catch in enough of your players to even it up. So you might have a big challenge ahead of you. Whatever you do, make sure you communicate with whoever is out there with you. This will help prevent your side from getting sniped while throwing, losing ball control, and other unpleasant things.

One thing to consider during endgame is what to do if it's down to you and just one other person on your side. If you only have one ball, and the other player on your team is more likely to catch balls or throw people out… it sucks sometimes to toss the only ball over to them, but it's better to put the team first in cases like this. Try and do what you can without a ball to swing the momentum. Like get a catch!

Lone Ranger Defense

If you're the last one in on your side, there's not much you can do sometimes. Especially if you suck at throwing. But you're not necessarily toast. Dodging and blocking are critical until you can get a catchable ball thrown your way. You can repeat that process until someone with an arm comes back into the game for your team. If you're a good enough blocker and dodger, you can eventually tire out their throwers. Then they will throw you something you can catch because they are gassed. Or they will make some other mistake.

TEAM LEADERSHIP

Being a leader on your dodgeball team is a lot like being a coach. There are a LOT of coach/players out there. Having good ones on your team can really help things. You don't have to be Phil Jackson out there to make a difference.

The Power of Your Voice

You may think it makes a difference, and you might not even think you're yelling at volume 11, but try not to blow everyone on your team's eardrums out with your in-game strategizing. Nobody likes to feel like they are being yelled at. That being said, there's nothing wrong with yelling out that your team has ball control, time to throw, watch out for that thrower over there, stuff like that.

Arguing Ref Calls

If there are refs for the game, be assertive yet courteous to them. You can actually help them call a better game by identifying things the other team (or its individual players seem to be doing. You can definitely state your case if it's obvious they made a wrong call, but give them the opportunity to explain their call.

Know The Rules

It's your job as a team captain/coach to ensure that your team knows how to play according to the rules of whatever league you're in. You won't know what strategy is best to use unless you know the parameters of the match. So read the rules inside and out.

**DODGECHANICS
PRO TIP**

**IF YOU KNOW THE RULES
BACKWARDS AND FORWARDS,
YOU WON'T LOOK LIKE AN ASS
WHEN YOU NEED TO CHALLENGE
A RULING ON THE COURT.**

Calling Timeout

If the league you play in allows you to call a timeout, remember to use it when you need it. The two best times to call timeout in dodgeball are when you feel the entire game's momentum has shifted and when you're winning a close game and the game's almost over.

Motivational Speeches

Before the match starts, between games, and during timeouts. Those are your opportunities to shine from a speaking perspective. I could write a whole book about what to tell your team in certain situations, but let's just say for now that it's part of the job whether you like it or not. And it makes a huge difference if you can look your teammates in the eyes and get them to rally around something you throw out there.

Starting a Rally Chant

One thing that's easy to do when you're a leader on your team is start up a chant from the outline, or even on court. Some teams employ a "go-to" chant that is based on the team name. Other easy ones to start are the last names of players who are still in the game. You can actually start a chant with any two or three syllable word. "Cline-bell! Cline-bell!" or "Pant-o-mime! Pant-o-mime!" See how easy it is?

Congratulate Good Play

Everyone appreciates being told they are doing a good job. It makes them want to do a good job more often. So when you see someone do something awesome, be the first to congratulate them. Giving thumbs up, saying "Hell yeah!" or high five are all ways of showing you are out to celebrate people doing good things for the team.

Lead By Example

Beware: your words can betray you if you don't act like you say. For example, if you tell people not to throw alone, don't do it yourself! Also, your actions are probably more influential than anything you actually say. If you play like a team player, your team will pick up on it. If you aren't a douche to anyone, they will likely follow.

CONGRATULATIONS

You've made it to the end of the book! It's time to crack open a beer (or something more age appropriate but equally refreshing). I hope you've learned a lot about dodgeball and laughed just as much along the way. If you'd like additional ninja tips, and to be a part of the book's community, please look up the title of the book "How To Play Dodgeball" with your favorite search engine or social media app. I look forward to seeing you there, and perhaps also on the court. Until next time.

THANKS

First off I thank whatever force is out there - I still have no idea how it works but am blessed by it nonetheless. I think the creative spark that ignited this project and the enduring flame that burns through long after its completion, it all comes from that unnamed but endless power.

That said, certainly this book would not have been possible without the help of so many awesome people. Apologies in advance to anyone I forgot to directly mention here.

Biggest thanks to my family. Sarah you're the best sister a guy could ask for. I laugh so much every day from the lifetime worth of silly inside jokes we have. You help me remember what's important and not to take life so seriously. I'm sure you're glad I didn't have access to a dodgeball when I was young to throw at you! Mom, thanks for being a beacon of creative light throughout my life. Thanks to my dad, who wrote a lot of books that unfortunately were never finished or published. I'm sure he'd be happy to see the Clinebell family name on a sports book cover. And to my grandparents and Uncle Gary, who have supported me beyond my wildest dreams with open hearts. You also taught me toughness, which is something you need a lot of to recover from some of the nasty injuries I've had playing dodgeball and other sports over the years. Jeff and Connor, my nephews, I love you both to death and snark with you every moment along the way. And to Deanna, my half-sister, I'm so glad I finally got the chance to meet you and your family. I'm so grateful we're all connected now - feels so good that the family got a bit bigger.

A million thanks to Beth Sass, Jessica Star, Jesse Soto, Bryan Neustein, Jay Turetzky, Brad Hagoski, Gina DiNapoli, Dave Benedetto, and Mark Hardy. All of you are dodgeball players, and I couldn't be prouder that your knowledgeable feedback and hard work has shaped this book into the rich resource it is. Mindi White, you did an awesome job proofreading and editing the copy. Greg Gubi, you got the layout done (a Herculean effort) and provided so much more than that in terms of marketing wisdom and helping me get the book out into the world and otherwise off the ground.

Much love to the dozens and dozens of dodgeball teams I've played on, from Winner Winner Chicken Dinner to the Knights Who Say "Ni!", from Aballo 13 to Death Throw Records. And including a few other personal favorites: Donkey Punches of Goats, The Motherfuckin' Rads, Jurassic Bark and Now That's What I Call Dodging, Volume 7.

Here's just a small fraction of the other players I've enjoyed the game of dodgeball with over the years. I have deep gratitude to all of you for teaching me so much about the game through your inspired play. You also happen to be endlessly hilarious and interesting people with huge hearts. The sport is lucky to have you in it. In no particular order: Michael Costanza, Andy Luster, Justin Hill, Sum Sum Chan, Erik Tillmans, Ish Blanco, Jesse Guberman, Howard Han, Jake Mason, Nevin Densham, James Monge, Ray Quinto, Cletus Ganschow, Malcolm Smith, Dani Shoenecker, Louise Palmieri, Jessica Sison, Myleen DeJesus, Mary-Jo Apigo, Kristin Caiella, Dani Goon, Simba Alvarado, David O'Brien, Vince Marchbanks, Michael Baisa, Michelle Murphy, Morris May, Daniel Schutz, Ryan Haley, Patrick Dodough, Rama Davis, Cory Meyerkord, Rahim Hodge, Paul Guest, Mark Kneyse, Matt Abrams, Ethan Brown, Alan Matkovic, Nic Ronga, Ryan Haley, Julia Muro, Nikil Nagaraj, Jared Almoro,

Drew Marlowe, Todd Daugherty, Heather Lee, Ashtar Goldreich, Colin Rothschild, Terrence and Tim Murphy, James Perry, Jim Sarratori and Michael Wilsker.

And special thanks to those players and friends I've had the most intense/fun one-on-one battles with: Brian Roth, Quinn Feldman, Dave Garcia, Gary Suggett, Tom Verrette, Alex Belciano, Josh Reitz, and Chris Alves.

Jon Hauer (JRock), Maxwell Mattord.. all I gotta say is Brobiotics for life. Bros get woke!

And here are a few more people who I'm eternally grateful for the support of, in dodgeball or otherwise. Thanks for helping make my life so great: Clay Campbell, Tony Barnstone, Alessio Miraglia, Stefano Bussadori, Mooka Rennick, Elliott Samuel Lemberger, Bill Lefler, Zak Shaffer, Brandon Herman, Sacha Sacket, Victoria Scott & Alfonso Rodenas, Jason Lowrie, Sam Knaak, Dario Forzato, Chelsea Aguilar, Chelsea Davis, Shani Kfir, Steve Collom, Lindsay Garfield, Sonnet Simmons, AG, Adrian Alvarado, Jadea Kelly, Lita Penaherrera, Doug Fenske, Melinda Hill, Sloane Kanter, Rich Jacques, Diallo Jackson, Jonathan Menchin, Erin Miller, Lolly Allen, Chase Rossner, Mayuto Correa, Eddie Gray, Ariana Hall, Gabe Isaac, Rachel Weinstein, Al Machera, Doug Fenske, Peter Petro, Tim & Sue Rocke and last but *never* the least John Wolf.

IMAGE CREDITS

Photographs on pages 31 to 65 and page 95 by Jessica Star.

Top illustration on page 70 by Henry Hustave on Unsplash.

Photograph on page 71 by Simon Alexander on Unsplash.

Top illustration on page 72 by rawpixel on Unsplash.

Bottom illustration on page 72 by JJ Bell and C. Robinson See: bibliodyssey.blogspot.com/2012/07/jack-of-all-trades.html. This illustration appears here courtesy of Shelly Cohen and Tanya Schramm, who sent me scans from this 1900 book. Attribution 2.0 Generic (CC BY 2.0).

Photograph on page 74 by Isaac Moore on Unsplash.

Photograph of author on back cover by Brittany Rouse.

APPENDICES

Common DBall RULES Mods

There are infinite ways to play dodgeball and no uniform pro rules are set. These are some of the most common rules modifications you will see. So be prepared for any combination or variation of them.

Deflections

During its travel time through the air, a ball can deflect off multiple targets before it is dead. Rules are often created for these scenarios. An example of such a rule would be if a thrown ball hits one player, then hits another player, then lands on the ground, both players are out.

Attack Line

Once a player obtains a ball, they cannot throw at the other team right away. Usually they have to run back until they are behind what's commonly referred to as an attack line. After clearing the attack line, they are then free to throw at the other side.

Ball Control

Most games are played with an uneven number of balls so that ball control can be established. When one team has more balls than the other side, they are required to throw however many balls it takes to make it so that they have fewer balls than the other side. This is ball control.

Out of Bounds

You have to stay within the confines of the court while you are playing in a game. If you go out of bounds, you are out. Common exceptions are when you are retrieving a ball that rolls out of bounds.

Headshots

Many leagues disallow throws that hit people in the head. This can be enforced by making the person who gets hit in the head safe, or by making the person who threw the ball out.

Suicides

Some leagues will allow you to throw at the other side after leaping over the center line. You have to throw the ball before your feet touch the ground on the other side. This is considered a suicide since you'll be out regardless of what happens. Although some leagues actually reward the suiciding player if they get their target out. One final word on this: be careful not to cross the center line with your foot when you're making your leap over. Ref might call you out.

Goofy Games

Sometimes it's fun to abandon the regular rules of dodgeball. Try some of these goofy games.

Left-Handed

In this variation, you throw with the opposite arm you normally would. Right-handed throwers throw left handed and vice versa. Optional rule is that girls still throw with their natural hand (making them often the best players on the court in this game). Trust me, you will laugh a lot playing this. Just be careful not to throw your weaker arm out.

Dr. Dodgeball

In this game, each team designates a player as their "doctor." That player can "revive" players from the outline and bring them back into the game. The way they do this is by touching a cone that is set up on the opposite side of the outline. I usually set it up on the center line and have both teams use that as their "medicine bag." After the doctor touches the medicine bag, they can then run back to the outline and high-five one player back into the game. The doctor can revive as many players as they want in this fashion, but once they are out, no more players can come back into the game. The doctor cannot be revived. Catches get the thrower out, but do not bring a player back into the game.

Save the President

Each team designates one player as their president. Once your president is out, the game is over and the other team wins.

Protect the Bottle

You set up a big Gatorade bottle on each side of the court (in the center, maybe a few feet away from the back wall). Each team has to protect their bottle from being knocked over. Whoever's bottle gets knocked over first loses. If you touch or knock over your own bottle, the other side automatically wins. You can't completely block the bottle from the view of the refs.

Blindfolded

This is a fun little game. It's an eight-player game. Each team has two blind players. Blindfolds are tied around their heads so they can't see. Each team has two guides. The only people who can throw are the blind players. The guides help the blind players aim their throws and avoid danger. Once the guides are out, they can still coach from the outline. The first team to eliminate the other completely wins.

Dodgeball Gear

The bottom line is: balance personal style with the need to keep your body in the correct number of pieces.

It's great—dodgeballers tend to treat their bodies like a Hello Kitty sticker store. Don't wear too much stuff, though, 'cause clothes count as your body. Although he could out-strafe anyone, MC Hammer was a terrible player because of his pants! Some people play close to nude. I wouldn't suggest it 'cause the ball hurts more when it hits bare skin and it can be a lot harder to catch. And people will curse you for turning the ball into a rubber sweat rag.

I guarantee that if you play long enough, you will eventually buy knee pads. Buy them now and save yourself the skid-burned caps. A lot of players also use compression sleeves on their arms and elbows. And some wear ankle braces. I kinda look like a tank when I'm out there with all my protective stuff. Works for me. Depending on how well you physically hold up, you can prolly do without a lot of it. I hear indoor wrestling shoes and soccer shoes work well for dodgeball. Can't say I've (successfully) tried anything but different varieties of basketball shoe. Regular athletic tape is a gift from God. You use it to tape the tips of your fingers so that you can grip the ball better. You can even reverse the final layer of tape so that your fingers literally stick to the ball.

Dodgeball Team Names

Puns are always a safe bet. Put "ball" or "balls" somewhere in your team name. Examples:
- The Good, the Bad, and the Ballsy
- Balls 'R' Us
- 2 Balls 1 Face

Random team name generators on the interwebs can be a source of great inspiration. For instance, Fat Punch Mafia.

Popular YouTube videos or Instagram memes can be referenced in or be the entire basis of your team name. Examples:
- Double Rainbow
- Dem Bois
- Boaty McBoatface

Movies, TV shows, music... there's enough pop culture out there to name a new team every ten seconds for a million years.

Unpopular political figure in your team name. Osama Bin Dodgin'. Awesome.

Setting Up The Gym for a Game

Basketball gyms are easily turned into dodgeball courts. Larger gyms can be split up into multiple games at once. You can get out the volleyball posts they have at the gym and run a six-foot tall net across the length of the court. That keeps the two games split up well.

Really small gyms are probably too small to split in half but can easily host one game. The only snag sometimes is needing to put a net in front of the gym stage. A lot of gym stages have curtains that you can close though, and that can act as a net.

Other preparations include taping lines with blue painter's tape (it's expensive but will lift easily and won't leave shitty residue on the court after the games). Common lines you will need to tape are the center line, attack lines, sidelines, and sometimes even the backline.

Dodgeball Stereotypes

This list was provided to me by the one and only "Super" Dave Benedetto.

The way a person plays dodgeball is who they are in life.

Lawyer – Argues every call.

Librarian – Keeps telling everyone to calm down.

IT Guy – Always goes for your balls. If he's not gonna get laid, you aren't either.

Bronze Medaler – Overly aggressive, doesn't really win.

Stock Broker/Insurance Salesman – They stand in front as if they are going to protect you, then dodge when the ball comes.

Baseball Players, Paper Boys, and Subpoena Servers – All accurate throwers.

Plumber – Crouching down constantly and exposing their ass crack.

Subway Sandwich Artist/Little Caesar's Pizza Maker (any food job requiring the quick assembly of menu items with many toppings) – Dodging sideways constantly.

Prisoner – Pump fakes constantly. Warding off potential shower comrades.

Additional Dodgeball Practice Drills

Dodging Drills

Dodgebox – You tape a 4' X 4' box on the court near a wall. You have throwers line up in a single-file line on the other side of the court. Each player takes a one-minute turn inside the dodgebox. When the whistle is blown, the throwers constantly take turns throwing at the player inside the dodgebox. The player inside the dodgebox is not allowed to catch any ball. They are to dodge everything thrown at them. Each time they are hit, or land outside of the dodgebox when dodging a throw, they get one point. Whoever gets the fewest number of points in a minute wins the round. BTW, throwers shag a ball and return to the back of the line after doing so to throw again.

Frogger – You split the back line of the court up into five segments using pieces of tape. Throwers stand on the other side. One dodger becomes the "frog," stepping into the first segment of the court. They slowly cross the court. They cannot move into the next segment of the court until they dodge at least one ball. They cannot catch a ball. The point is to dodge better. If they are hit, they have to start over. Throwers are allowed to throw more than one ball at a time, but don't all throw at once.

Contra Cheat Code – The NES game Contra had a cheat code that went up, up, down, down, left, right, left, right, B, A, Select, Start. You can do reps of the following dodge sequence: hop forward, jump in the air, hop backwards, duck, lean to the left (legs stay in place), lean to the right, strafe left, strafe right, crouch to the ground as low as you can go, then do a Mario Brothers super jump. Those are all the basic moves of dodging!

Catching Drills

Styles Drill

Get a throwing partner. Each time they throw at you, alternate to a different catching technique (regardless of how it looks like they are throwing at you): breadbasket catch, hands catch, one-handed grab, catching while kneeling on the ground, etc. This will give you more versatility.

Count to Twenty

Count with your throwing partner as you throw back and forth. Each catch you add a number to your count. If one of you drops a catch, you start over. Count until you hit twenty. Repeat as desired.

Fake 'N' Catch

With this drill, you have a ball. You act like you are throwing at an imaginary target, then stop mid-motion, drop the ball, and turn at a 45° angle assuming a catching stance. Repeat this down the length of the court and back. This prepares you to bait people into throwing at you as you are throwing and makes you mentally prepared to make a catch on their snipe attempt.

Throwing Drills

Wall Snipe

You stand maybe eight or ten feet away from the wall and throw the ball so that it hits the wall about a foot off the ground. The ball will rebound back to you. Do this repeatedly. You can get into a rhythm with it. This is perfect for practicing foot snipes close to the line.

Line Fault Drill

The closer you are to your target, the faster your throw will be when it reaches them and the less time they will have to react. So you want to practice throwing right up to the center line without crossing it. You can tape a line or use a line already on the court. Don't concentrate as much on your throw. Pay more attention to your footwork and not crossing the line. Try to get as close as you can. Before long, you will be aware of the center line without having to look.

Dodgebowling

You can set up plastic bowling pins or just get some empty Vitamin Water bottles and line them up across the court. Then knock them down!

Reffing Tips

These are my CliffsNotes on reffing dodgeball games, having crewed on probably a thousand of them.

Know the Rules

This seems like a "no duh," but you'd be surprised how often refs make a call based on bad info. When you have a whistle, the players look to you as the living rules book. Also, if you don't know the rules, savvy players can manipulate the game to their advantage. Which can result in more player arguments when your enforcement isn't up to par.

Call Only What You See

Refs are going to make bad calls 25% of the time, correct calls 25% of the time, and are simply not going to see the other 50% because so many things are happening at once. Since there's no multicamera replay available, you can't make a call you don't see with your own eyes. If you make calls you think may have happened, you will make a lot of bad calls. If you only call the things you are certain happened, people will respect you. Remember, the honor code will shame a lot of people who know they got hit into excusing themselves from the action if you just look in their direction without making a call. That will happen a lot of times when I'm not sure if I saw someone get hit, then give the player in question a look that suggests "I saw that. You should go out if you were hit."

Assert Yourself

Dodgeball games are loud. There's thundering music and players yelling stuff all the time. And players are focused on the game, not on you. So if you decide to call someone out, do it with authority. Point at them, (lightly) blow your whistle, and signal they are out once you have their attention. That is the ideal sequence: point, get attention, then communicate. Sometimes you will have to stop the game altogether to get someone to notice you and honor your call. This is fine.

Stick to Your Call

Once you make a call, the worst thing you can do is cave to someone who either ignores you or argues against it. It makes you look weak and then no one will respect your calls. The only times you should reconsider your call is when another ref says they had a better angle on the action, or if upon discussion with the players it is totally obvious you made the wrong call.

Remain Calm

People get agitated out there. Sometimes they yell swears at each other, make obscene hand gestures, and even occasionally resort to physical violence. It's best to keep yourself out of the drama as much as possible by keeping a level head no matter what. Nothing will lose you the respect of the players faster than being a jerk. And it also gives them the impression you endorse that kind of behavior yourself.

Keep Track

If you have a stopwatch you're supposed to use, keep an eye on it. If you mark down on a clipboard every time a team wins a game in a match, don't forget that. If the teams alternate ball control each game, try and remember who had ball control last. Being accountable for your duties will reduce your stress and player bitching.

Additional Tips for All The Wonder Women

I know what some ladies might be saying. "Super lame to make a special section of the book for us. We can read the rest of the book like guys can, thank you very much!" I completely acknowledge and respect that perspective. If you feel that way, feel free to pretend this section doesn't exist and accept my sincere apology.

This appendix is in the book because the honest truth is that it can be intimidating to step onto a dodgeball court as a lady. I can say this confidently because I've heard it directly from the mouths of dozens of women when they begin to play dodgeball.

I have a few tips to share that will get you going and will *especially* help you develop your own set of superpowers on the court. Trust me that some of the most enthusiastic and talented players in coed leagues are women, but many of them will tell you that it didn't happen overnight. Some of them were completely terrified of the game when they started out.

First off, if you are completely new to the game, I suggest picking one skill to work on at first. Catching and/or simply dodging are great skills to start with. Know that some of the best catchers in the leagues I've played in are women. Use the instructional sections of this book for whatever skill you want to develop. Then the longer you play and apply proven techniques, the more you will grow as a player. Once you've learned one skill, then you can evaluate what to learn from there.

Have an open mind about what you might be good at on the court, but don't deny your natural talents. Make sure to play to your unique strengths. No one is made the same. Some ladies have stronger arms than others. Others might never be great throwers but could become epic catchers and team leaders.

When learning to throw (and it's a good practice in general anyways), find a friend to throw with.. It's a lot easier to get someone out when they have to dodge two balls instead of just one.

If you find yourself behind someone during a game, move. Full court vision is key. Ladies tend to be smaller than guys and so being in the back exacerbates sight loss. Just shift a little to the left or a little to the right so you can see everything clearly at all times.

Move all the way up to the line before throwing. It can be scary to move up all the way to center of the court, but guess what: the throwing distance gets significantly shorter. As a result, when you let it rip from that place, your throws will be stronger and more accurate.

Always aim low! Might as well get out a highlighter and accent this one. This is probably the #1 reason ladies get their throws caught. Low throws are much harder to catch.

Don't forget to just be yourself and have fun out there too. The coed leagues would not be the same without all the diva energy expressed out there during the games. Girls know how to lighten things up just as much as they know how to kick ass!

Finally, it's worth looking into all-female leagues in your area. Even the leagues that don't offer that will often host all-female events like clinics that are designed to help new lady players meet each other and learn from local female rockstars.

GLOSSARY

"DODGEBALLISMS"

ATTACK LINE - the line you must cross behind before you are allowed to throw a ball during the opening rush.

BALL CONTROL - the concept of actively managing the number of balls your team controls at any given time throughout the game so you are never at a large disadvantage.

BLOCKING - using a ball you are holding to deflect an incoming throw.

CENTER LINE - the horizontal line that runs directly in between the two teams on the court.

COUNTDOWN - an audible countdown typically used to synchronize throws.

CROSSCOURT THROW - throwing at an opponent at an acute angle, across the width of the court. An example of this is a thrower on the far left side of their side of the court throwing at an opponent who is on the other side but to the thrower's far right.

DEAD BALL - a ball that has hit a wall or the floor, or someone's head (in a lot of leagues). A dead ball no longer can be caught or get anyone out.

DEFLECTION - a live ball that has been blocked by a ball or has hit a player but still hasn't hit a wall or the floor.

FAST COUNTERS - throwing aggressively at an opponent immediately after they throw and are usually most vulnerable to attack.

HEADSHOT - a throw that directly hits an opponent in the head.

KILL LIST - a list of players you want to get out on the other team, usually ordered by the skill of the player (most skilled to least).

OPENING RUSH - the initial action that takes place when teams run for the balls at the center line at the start of a game of dodgeball.

OUT LINE a line up of players who are out of a dodgeball game. Each team has its own out line. It starts with the first player to get out and ends with the most recent player to get out.

PINCHING - forcibly gripping a ball in such a manner where "rubber meets rubber."

POP UP - a thrown ball that has been deflected high into the air.

PUMP FAKE - faking you are throwing at a target whether you have a ball or not.

REBOUNDS - thrown balls that miss their targets and bounce off the wall behind them.

RUNNERS - the players on your team who typically run for balls on the center line during the opening rush.

SHAGGING - legally going out of bounds to retrieve a ball. This term can also apply to collecting balls in play at the back of your side of the court.

SNIPE - attempting to throw out a vulnerable player, typically someone who isn't paying attention to you, or is in the middle of their throwing motion.

SUICIDE - jumping over the center line to throw a ball (while you are still in the air) at an opponent.

TURTLING - crouching down in a corner with a ball in a defensive posture. Can also be used to describe a defensive team strategy where you are all hunkering down for the worst and playing very conservatively.

NOTES:

NOTES:

HowToPlayDodgeball.com

Made in the USA
Middletown, DE
19 November 2018